SMART GUIDE

CRE▲TIVE
HOMEOWNER®

sheds
step-by-step

CREATIVE HOMEOWNER®, Upper Saddle River, New Jersey

COPYRIGHT © 2009

CRE🏠TIVE
HOMEOWNER®

A Division of Federal Marketing Corp.
Upper Saddle River, NJ

This book may not be reproduced, either in part or in its entirety, in any form, by any means, without written permission from the publisher, with the exception of brief excerpts for purposes of radio, television, or published review. All rights, including the right of translation, are reserved. Note: Be sure to familiarize yourself with manufacturer's instructions for tools, equipment, and materials before beginning a project. Although all possible measures have been taken to ensure the accuracy of the material presented, neither the author nor the publisher is liable in case of misinterpretation of directions, misapplication, or typographical error.

SMARTGUIDE® and Creative Homeowner® are resgistered trademarks of Federal Marketing Corp.

SMART GUIDE: SHEDS

AUTHORS	John D. Wagner, Bill Hylton
GRAPHIC DESIGNER	Kathryn Wityk
MANAGING EDITOR	Fran Donegan
JUNIOR EDITOR	Jennifer Calvert
EDITORIAL ASSISTANT	Sara Markowitz
TECHNICAL EDITOR	Steve Willson
PHOTO COORDINATOR	Mary Dolan
DIGITAL IMAGING SPECIALIST	Frank Dyer
INDEXER	Schroeder Indexing Services
SMART GUIDE® SERIES COVER DESIGN	Clarke Barre
FRONT COVER PHOTOGRAPHY	Andrew Kline

CREATIVE HOMEOWNER

VICE PRESIDENT AND PUBLISHER	Timothy O. Bakke
MANAGING EDITOR	Fran J. Donegan
ART DIRECTOR	David Geer
PRODUCTION COORDINATOR	Sara M. Markowitz

Current Printing (last digit)
10 9 8 7 6 5 4 3 2 1

Manufactured in the United States of America

Smart Guide: Sheds, First Edition
Library of Congress Control Number: 2008934558
ISBN-10: 1-58011-439-3
ISBN-13: 978-1-58011-439-4

CREATIVE HOMEOWNER®
A Division of Federal Marketing Corp.
24 Park Way
Upper Saddle River, NJ 07458
www.creativehomeowner.com

Metric Conversion

Length

1 inch	25.4 mm
1 foot	0.3048 m
1 yard	0.9144 m
1 mile	1.61 km

Area

1 square inch	645 mm^2
1 square foot	0.0929 m^2
1 square yard	0.8361 m^2
1 acre	4046.86 m^2
1 square mile	2.59 km^2

Volume

1 cubic inch	16.3870 cm^3
1 cubic foot	0.03 m^3
1 cubic yard	0.77 m^3

Common Lumber Equivalents

Sizes: Metric cross sections are so close to their U.S. sizes, as noted below, that for most purposes they may be considered equivalents.

Dimensional lumber	1 x 2	19 x 38 mm
	1 x 4	19 x 89 mm
	2 x 2	38 x 38 mm
	2 x 4	38 x 89 mm
	2 x 6	38 x 140 mm
	2 x 8	38 x 184 mm
	2 x 10	38 x 235 mm
	2 x 12	38 x 286 mm
Sheet sizes	4 x 8 ft.	1200 x 2400 mm
	4 x 10 ft.	1200 x 3000 mm
Sheet thicknesses	¼ in.	6 mm
	⅜ in.	9 mm
	½ in.	12 mm
	¾ in.	19 mm
Stud/joist spacing	16 in. o.c.	400 mm o.c.
	24 in. o.c.	600 mm o.c.

Capacity

1 fluid ounce	29.57 mL
1 pint	473.18 mL
1 quart	1.14 L
1 gallon	3.79 L

Weight

1 ounce	28.35g
1 pound	0.45kg

Temperature

Celsius = Fahrenheit − 32 x ⁵⁄₉
Fahrenheit = Celsius x 1.8 + 32

Nail Size & Length

Penny Size	Nail Length
2d	1"
3d	1¼ in.
4d	1½ in.
5d	1¾ in.
6d	2 in.
7d	2¼ in.
8d	2½ in.
9d	2¾ in.
10d	3"
12d	3¼ in.
16d	3½ in.

contents

safety first

Though all the designs and methods in this book have been reviewed for safety, it is not possible to overstate the importance of using the safest construction methods possible. What follows are reminders; some do's and don'ts of basic carpentry. They are not substitutes for your own common sense.

- *Always* use caution, care, and good judgment when following the procedures described in this book.

- *Always* be sure that the electrical setup is safe; be sure that no circuit is overloaded and that all power tools and electrical outlets are properly grounded. Do not use power tools in wet locations.

- *Always* read container labels on paints, solvents, and other products; provide ventilation, and observe all other warnings.

- *Always* read the manufacturer's instructions for using a tool, especially the warnings.

- *Always* use hold-downs and push sticks whenever possible when working on a table saw. Avoid working short pieces if you can.

- *Always* remove the key from any drill chuck (portable or press) before starting the drill.

- *Always* pay deliberate attention to how a tool works so that you can avoid being injured.

- *Always* know the limitations of your tools. Do not try to force them to do what they were not designed to do.

- *Always* make sure that any adjustment is locked before proceeding. For example, always check the rip fence on a table saw or the bevel adjustment on a portable saw before starting to work.

- *Always* clamp small pieces firmly to a bench or other work surface when using a power tool on them.

- *Always* wear the appropriate rubber or work gloves when handling chemicals, moving or stacking lumber, or doing heavy construction.

- *Always* wear a disposable face mask when you create dust by sawing or sanding. Use a special filtering respirator when working with toxic substances and solvents.

- *Always* wear eye protection, especially when using power tools or striking metal on metal or concrete; a chip can fly off, for example, when chiseling concrete.

- *Always* be aware that there is seldom enough time for your body's reflexes to save you from injury from a power tool in a dangerous situation; everything happens too fast. Be *alert!*

- *Always* keep your hands away from the business ends of blades, cutters, and bits.

- *Always* hold a circular saw firmly, usually with both hands so that you know where they are.

- *Always* use a drill with an auxiliary handle to control the torque when large-size bits are used.

- *Always* check your local building codes when planning new construction. The codes are intended to protect public safety and should be observed to the letter.

- *Never* work with power tools when you are tired or under the influence of alcohol or drugs.

- *Never* cut tiny pieces of wood or pipe using a power saw. Cut small pieces off larger pieces.

- *Never* change a saw blade or a drill or router bit unless the power cord is unplugged. Do not depend on the switch being off; you might accidentally hit it.

- *Never* work in insufficient lighting.

- *Never* work while wearing loose clothing, hanging hair, open cuffs, or jewelry.

- *Never* work with dull tools. Have them sharpened, or learn how to sharpen them yourself.

- *Never* use a power tool on a workpiece—large or small—that is not firmly supported.

- *Never* saw a workpiece that spans a large distance between horses without close support on each side of the cut; the piece can bend, closing on and jamming the blade, causing saw kickback.

- *Never* support a workpiece from underneath with your leg or other part of your body when sawing.

- *Never* carry sharp or pointed tools, such as utility knives, awls, or chisels, in your pocket. If you want to carry such tools, use a special-purpose tool belt with leather pockets and holders.

introduction

Building a Shed

Everyone could use a little more storage space, right? If you are like most homeowners, your garage, basement, or crawl space—or maybe all three—are filled to the brim with the lawn mowers, tools, snow-removal equipment, and other gadgets you need to keep your home functioning properly. Some of those items are only used a few times each year; others you may reach for on a regular basis. But no matter how often they are used, they all take up valuable space.

A yard and garden shed offers a chance for you to cut some of that clutter—or at least organize it in a way that makes sense. A shed is an inexpensive storage alternative that is relatively easy to design and build, and it can improve the look and value of your property.

Smart Guide: Sheds provides the inspiration and the how-to instruction to help you add a shed to your yard. The book approaches the shed-acquiring experience from a number of different angles. This introduction lays out some of the tasks you will need to perform, including selecting the style and size that meets your needs, deciding on a place for your shed, and adhering to building codes.

This shed is used as a potting shed.

But this book is about building your own shed, and Chapters 1 through 3 lay the groundwork for tackling a shed-building project on your own. These chapters cover the tools you will need and basic construction techniques on foundations and framing. There is even a section on adding electrical power to your shed.

The last three chapters are a guide to actually building custom sheds. The author created the designs and then went to work constructing the buildings. Photographers followed the progress of the author/builders so that you can see how the projects went from empty spaces to ones occupied by attractive, useful outbuildings. Each project includes a list of materials, a diagram showing how the parts of the sheds go together, and dozens of step-by-step photographs that detail the building process. Each author describes what he did and why, and there are Smart Tips throughout to help you with your project. You can use the authors' designs as guides to

build your own shed, although you should adjust measurements to suit your needs. Or you can create your own design.

Shed Designs. There is a garden shed here for everyone, no matter what the storage needs or the skill level of the builder. The Saltbox Shed, page 48, is the largest and most complex project. It measures 12 x 16 feet and features two large doors, a saltbox roof, and cedar siding.

The Gambrel Shed, page 74, has the appearance of a small barn. It can provide ample storage for lawn and garden equipment. You can easily convert the upper area to an additional storage area.

The Gable Shed, page 90, can hold tools or be used as a potting shed. The classic gable roof and cedar shingle siding make it an attractive addition to any yard.

People build sheds for a variety of reasons. So whether you want to increase storage space, need a potting shed to make gardening easier, or you want to tackle a building project for the joy of working with your hands, it is time to get started.

Choosing a Shed Design

The term "shed" has come to include a number of different types of buildings. While most people think of a shed as a place to store tools and equipment, a shed can also be the building in the garden where you transplant plants, a hobby area, a workshop, a playhouse, or even a private place for relaxation. The first step in building a shed is to decide how you will use the building. Determining its intended use will help you pick the right size shed for your needs and for the limitations of your property.

The Right Size. With proper shelving, a shed that is 6 x 8 feet can store your power mover, a trimmer, and a number of hand tools and garden supplies. But you may have to remove some of those items to reach the tool you want. When planning, consider the actual floor space each item will occupy along with enough room to navigate around the building. A rule of thumb is to leave a 12-inch buffer zone around equipment. If the shed will double as a work area, you'll need 36 inches or more between workspaces. For example, allow 8 feet on either end of a table saw. Some examples are shown below.

Shed Plans

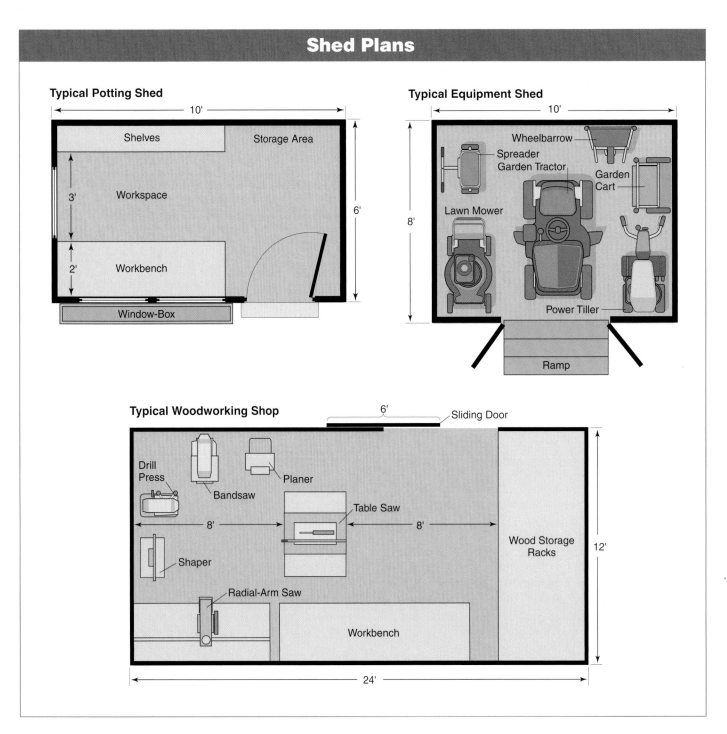

Rural areas usually don't have stringent building codes or restrictions on sheds. This structure is a focal point and a destination in a large garden.

The Right Site

The siting of the shed—where it is positioned on your property—will influence its size. For any location, there must be enough room to accommodate the foundation "footprint" of the shed with a border of clear ground around the perimeter, as the eaves will extend beyond the foundation by 12 to 18 inches. Moreover, the ground must be level, or it must be modified through excavation to be made level. The type of foundation you choose can also level the shed. So your dream location may not be the ideal spot to place your shed. You will need to consider the topography and local building codes.

Setbacks. For most suburban locations, you will likely need to comply with setback requirements. A setback is the minimum allowable distance between the structure you want to build and some other landmark, such as another building, the property line, the street, even an easement that is identified only on a deed. Setbacks can range up to 100 feet or more. Municipalities enact setbacks to regulate construction. Setbacks prevent property owners from building close to the street or a property line. Adhering to setbacks is no small matter. Violation of a setback is grounds for dismantling or moving your shed, so call your local building department to determine applicable setbacks for your property.

Use your shed as a chance to make a statement in your garden. You can copy the color scheme used on the main house or create something totally different.

If your plans don't comply with local setback or zoning laws, you can apply for a variance. Your application will be considered by the local zoning board or the building inspector. Inquire at the building department for zoning variance procedures.

Covenants. These are rules set by local communities, neighborhoods, or homeowner associations that can hold sway over aspects of your shed that might surprise you. There may be restrictive covenants that apply to the type of siding or color paint you can use. Check with your homeowner association to see what rules, if any, apply to garden shed construction. In addition to your local building permit authority, a homeowner association's architectural review board may want building plans and elevations (scale sketches of the shed as seen from the side) to review before approval can be granted to build a shed.

Zoning. These requirements may cover shed construction and what you can keep in it. Zoning can regulate everything from roof types—wood shake and shingle roofs are illegal in some fire-prone areas—to live animals. Goats or chickens may seem like a great idea, until you learn that your town bars you from keeping them. You may not even be allowed to have an "outbuilding," as sheds are called. So, early on in the planning stages, check with your town or city's building department for applicable codes and ordinances, and check with your homeowners association for any required architectural review.

Building Codes. In rural locations, building codes, as well as covenants and zoning regulations, may be less restrictive than those found in towns and cities. If you are building a shed on a 5- or 10-acre lot, local building codes and zoning may not impact your design at all. However, it is important to remember that building codes are good guidance for "best-practices" and minimum design standards when building any structure. Your municipality or building code authority—the city or town department that issues the building permit—will tell you the code to which you must adhere. Increasingly the International Building Code (IBO) is the standard that applies, but some counties, especially in hurricane- or tornado-prone areas, can demand that structures be beefed up beyond IBO requirements.

Building Permits and Inspections. Building permits are usually required for building any structure on your property. If a building permit is required and you don't have one, you may be asked to remove the shed, even long after it is built. However, for small structures you can usually obtain a building permit after the structure is erected and simply pay a fine or extra fee.

The requirements for building permits vary widely. Some towns and cities exempt structures that are built on nonpermanent foundations, such as concrete blocks or wood skids resting on gravel. If you must obtain a building permit, apply for one at your municipality's building department. The type of permit and fee you pay is usually related to the proposed square footage or cost of the shed.

You may need to provide rudimentary building plans and know your square footage. It may take a few days or a week for permit approval, and if you are asking for a

SMART TIP

Be present during the building inspections so that the inspector can tell you what needs to be done to get a "pass." Sometimes you can fix a problem while the inspector is there.

This custom structure boasts all the comforts of home.

zoning variance, your permit may take even longer and be subject to public notice and hearings. Investigate the building permit process early in your planning.

If you require a building permit, your shed will be subject to building inspections. Even though your shed may be a small structure, the building inspector may be called in to approve the foundation, electrical, and framing. You will also be required to get a final inspection once you complete the building. You may also get a "pass with condition," which requests that you make a fix that the inspector doesn't have to reinspect.

Choose a shed, right, based on how the building will be used. A place to store garden tools need not be as large as a woodshop.

chapter 1
tools & materials

Tools

Good tools can help you do a good job of building your shed or any type of building or outbuilding. You don't need to invest in top-of-the-line tools, but good-quality mid-priced tools will go a long way in helping you work efficiently and safely. This chapter discusses the basic tools you will need for this type of construction project, including tools for layout, cutting, attachment, and working safely. You will also learn how to select the right materials, including distinguishing from among the different types of lumber available.

Construction Levels

It is essential to build any structure plumb, level, and square. To do that, you will at least want to have a 4-foot spirit level for checking framing, and a line level and mason's string for checking long spans.

Spirit Levels. Spirit levels come in many lengths. A 4-foot model is best for working with framing. You can also extend its useful range by resting it on a long, straight 2x4.

Digital Levels. Unlike spirit levels, digital levels beep when they are level or plumb. The tools never go out of whack because you can reset them electronically. Some electronic levels also work as inclinometers to give you the angle of rafters. That feature can be handy when you have to match roof pitches in separate, distant locations.

Water Level. A water level is basically colored water in a long, clear tube with gradation marks on both ends. Because water seeks its own level no matter what the distance or terrain, you can use the tool for long-distance level checks. Once any air bubbles are removed, stretch the hose from one place to another (even up and down over rough terrain) and the water line at both ends will be level.

For grading sloped land and laying out level foundations, you'll need to use a transit, a builder's level, or a laser level. These tools allow you to sight a level line across large distances. These are expensive items, so you should rent them, if possible, when you're building from scratch.

Masonry Tools

Whether you're working with concrete, brick, or unit masonry (such as concrete block), you'll need many of the same basic masonry tools. You can easily rent many expensive items, so check before you buy a tool that you may not use often. You'll need trowels and floats for the placing and finishing of concrete, and a bull float (made of magnesium or steel) or a darby (made of wood) to finish the upper layer of curing concrete. With a finishing trowel, you can create a smooth surface once the concrete is leveled; then you'll use edging and jointing trowels on the surface of the smooth concrete. An edging trowel makes a rounded edge on a concrete slab, which is safer and more durable than a sharp edge. A groover has a ridge down the center of its blade to form grooves or control joints. Jointers are metal rods (round or square) attached to a handle that you use to create various mortar joints when working with brick and concrete block.

Spirit levels are indispensable tools for carpentry. A 4-ft. level is needed for many aspects of framing and finishing; smaller levels are good for doors and windows.

Digital levels are used much like spirit levels, but they have a digital readout. Most will emit a beep when level or plumb.

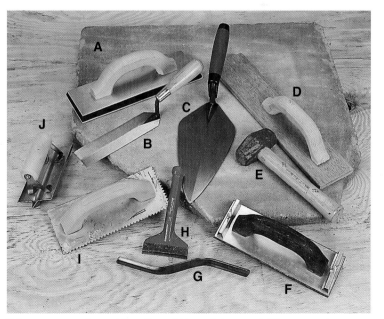

Masonry tools: rubber float (A), striking tool (B), mason's trowel (C), wood float (D), 5-lb. hammer (E), magnesium float (F), jointer (G), brickset (H), notched trowel (I), and groover (J).

Driving Nails & Screws

Hammers. Pros often use a 20- to 24-ounce waffle-head, or serrated, straight-claw framing hammer. Wooden (hickory) handles tend to absorb vibration better than fiberglass handles, so some people think wooden handles lessen your chances of developing repetitive motion ailments such as carpal tunnel syndrome. If you're not used to manual labor, a 24-ounce hammer may be too heavy for you, and you'll probably be better off with the 20- or 16-ounce size.

Nail Gun. A pneumatic, or air-driven, nail gun, which uses a magazine that holds up to 100 or more nails, can take much of the tedium out of repetitive nailing. But you pay a price: nail guns are expensive and heavy, and you need compressors and hoses to run them. Nail guns really don't pay for themselves—purchased or rented—unless you have a great amount of nailing to do all at one time.

Most guns handle 6d through 16d nails. You'll need a compressor, gasoline or electric, and at least 100 feet of air hose. If you can, go with the quieter electric compressor. Also, make sure you set the compressor's in-line regulator to the pressure required for the tool you'll be using.

Power Drill. A corded or battery-powered drill is essential not only for driving wood screws but also for quickly and precisely drilling holes. If cost is an issue, buy a plug-in, heavy-duty, ⅜-inch drill with variable speeds. If you can afford the extra cost, you'll find a cordless drill even handier. Cordless drills come in an array of voltage ratings; the higher the voltage, the more powerful the drill. A 12-volt drill generally is powerful enough to fill all your needs.

Squares

For accurate layout, you'll need a framing square. It's etched for layout of plumb and seat cuts for common

Cordless tools are great for shed building, especially if you are working away from an electrical receptacle. Buy an extra battery so that your tool will be ready whenever you are.

rafters or hip rafters, plus degrees of angle for use as a protractor. A speed square—a heavy-duty aluminum right triangle—is great for guiding your saw and marking lumber, and also is etched with information. A combination square and a sliding T-bevel are helpful in marking cut lines on framing.

Framing Square. A framing square is an L-shaped tool made of steel or aluminum. It is indispensable when cutting rafters, marking cut lines on lumber, and making sure corners are square. Like the speed square, the framing square has figures etched into it. The figures sometimes include extensive rafter tables.

Combination Square. A combination square is a ruler with a sliding bracket mounted to it at 90 degrees. The bracket has a second surface, which you can use to make 45-degree cut lines on lumber. Some squares have a pointed metal scribe to mark work for cutting. This tool is handy, but the speed square will serve most of your needs.

Sliding T Bevel Gauge. Often called a bevel square or bevel gauge, this tool is useful for some complicated framing problems. You can set a sliding T bevel gauge at any angle and use it to transfer the same angle from one place to another.

A framing square is a useful tool for checking stud layout, squaring up corners, and marking long cuts. For roof framing, a framing square with rafter tables is a useful addition to your tool kit.

A combination square has a sliding blade, for making short measurements, checking right angles, and marking lumber cuts. Some have a spirit level.

Other Basic Tools

Drill Bits. The standard twist drill bit bores holes in wood, plastic, or metal. Spade bits quickly make large holes in wood, but not as cleanly as other bits. Masonry bits drill holes into brick and concrete. Hole saws make large, accurate holes up to several inches in diameter. Single-twist auger bits have a small cone-shaped point at the tip to make them more accurate than traditional bits. Forstner bits cut holes with very little tear-out. An adjustable screw pilot bit will stop at a predetermined depth and cut a countersink all in one step.

Wrenches and Pliers. Combination wrenches, adjustable wrenches, nut drivers, and socket wrenches have count-less applications. You'll use pipe and spud wrenches when working with plumbing. For wiring, electrician's pliers, the multipurpose tool, and the cable ripper come in handy. Slip joint, diagonal-cutting, and needle-nose pliers have many practical uses.

Woodworking Tools. Use a tool belt when carrying nails and screws. Sanders, planes, and files help even out surfaces. Use measuring tapes to lay out the site and measure for cuts. Use knives and chisels to cut small amounts of material in places where a saw is not practical. You can use a pry bar as a lever in a variety of building situations. A screwdriver is often the only practical means of driving a screw.

This basic collection includes a standard twist drill bit (A), spade bit (B), masonry bit (C), hole saw (D), single-twist auger bit (E), Forstner bit (F), and adjustable screw pilot bit (G).

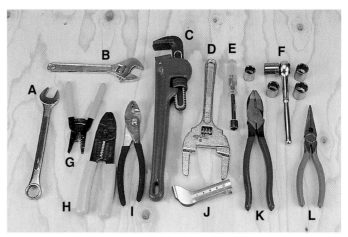

Wrenches: combination (A), adjustable (B), pipe (C), spud (D), nut driver (E), socket (F); pliers: electrician's (G), multipurpose tool (H), slip-joint (I), cable stripper (J), cutting (K), and needle-nose (L).

A socket wrench kit or a set of combination wrenches is necessary for driving nuts onto bolts. For some jobs, you will need extra-deep sockets and an extended handle.

Woodworking tools: tool belt (A), belt sander (B), smooth plane (C), scraper (D), long reel-type tape (E), screwdrivers (F), utility knife (G), measuring tape (H), sandpaper (I), wood chisels (J), wood files (K), and a pry bar (L).

Using Saws Safely

Set up a safe cutting station on heavy-duty boards or thick plywood fastened to sturdy sawhorses on level ground. When you cut large pieces, you must have something to support the wood that's hanging in midair; otherwise, it will droop and bind your cut, increasing the risk of kickback.

Kickback happens when a blade binds in the cut or the teeth try to take too much of a bite, and the saw jumps back at you. It happens quickly and is quite dangerous. You can buy antikickback blades, which have modified tooth designs, but you can best reduce kickback by not rushing a cut and by stabilizing your work. Always stay away from directly behind the saw, and don't remove the saw from the workpiece until the blade has stopped.

When cutting wood where you'll install it, support the wood, preferably on sawhorses. Keep your hands as far as possible from the cut, and clearly sight your cut line to make sure it's free of obstructions such as nails or extension cords. Firmly place wood on a cutting surface; never cut wood held in your hand.

Saws

Though framing doesn't demand the precise cuts that finish carpentry does, you still need high-quality saws with sharp blades. With power saws, a 7¼-inch circular saw is a practical choice. Look for one with good balance that is light enough for you to maneuver and easy to adjust for angle and depth. Make sure it has a comfortable handle.

A table saw also adds tremendous capability to a project because you can rip sheets of plywood and boards quickly and accurately.

Handsaws. Crosscut saws are versatile handsaws about 24 inches long, with seven or eight teeth per inch. You can also buy specialized trim saws and rip saws.

You'll need a variety of handsaws for framing and finish work: crosscut saws are useful for making cuts where it's impractical to maneuver a circular saw.

A 7¼-in. mid-priced circular saw is the best model for most do-it-yourselfers. Battery-powered models are available for sites located far from a source of electricity.

Backsaws—shorter, stiffer, and broader than crosscut saws and with finer teeth—are good for detail and trimwork. Hacksaws are essential for cutting pipe, nails, and other materials too tough for a wood saw. Keyhole saws have a narrow-point blade handy for making small cutouts; stubbier versions with coarser teeth are called utility saws and are good for cutting outlet and other openings in drywall. Coping saws are used mainly to join curved-profile moldings.

Circular Saw. A circular saw is capable of quickly cross-cutting, ripping, and beveling boards or sheets of plywood. The most popular saws are those that take a 7¼-inch blade. With this blade size you can cut to a maximum depth of about 2½ inches at 90 degrees. Some contractors use circular saws with larger blades for cutting posts in one pass, but a 7¼-inch circular saw is easier to control, and it allows you to cut anything as large as a 6x6 with a second pass. Smaller saws are also available, some of which are battery powered. These saws are often referred to as trim saws. Battery-driven models can be useful in situations when extension cords would get in the way.

Don't judge power saw performance by horsepower rating alone. Also look at the amperage that the motor draws. Low-cost saws may have 9- or 10-amp motors with drive shafts and arbors running on rollers or sleeve bearings. A contractor-grade saw generally is rated at 12 or 13 amps and is made with more-durable ball bearings. Plastic housings are no longer the mark of an inferior tool; however, a flimsy base plate made of stamped metal is. A thin base won't stay as flat as an extruded or cast base. To minimize any chance of electric shock, be sure that your saw is double insulated. Most saws have a safety switch that you must depress before the trigger will work.

Reciprocating Saw. This saw comes in handy for cutting rough openings in sheathing, fixing framing errors, cutting nail-embedded wood, or cutting the last ½ inch that your circular saw can't get to when you cut to a perpendicular line. Buy plenty of wood- and metal-cutting blades, but don't confuse the two. Wood blades have larger, more-offset teeth than the small-toothed metal-cutting blades.

Power Miter Saw. For angle cuts, you'll want to use a power miter saw, also called a chop saw. This tool is simply a circular saw mounted on a pivot assembly, which enables you to make precise straight and angled crosscuts in boards. You can buy chop saws that handle 10- to 15-inch blades. A 12-inch saw is often the best value for the money. Use a 60-tooth combination-cut carbide blade for all around work.

A reciprocating saw, used for making rough cuts, is good for demolition work. It's also handy for cutting openings for a window, door, or roof vent.

SMART TIP

Working safely with cutting tools is a matter of common sense. Always wear goggles when making cuts; pay attention to the work at hand; and unplug power saws when changing blades.

A power miter saw may be the right choice to speed up your production if you don't have enough room for a table or radial-arm saw in the work area.

Lumber

Wood is one of the most important materials you'll buy for your project, so you should purchase the best quality you can afford.

Hardwood & Softwood

Wood is generally divided into two broad categories: hardwood and softwood. Common hardwoods include ash, birch, cherry, poplar, black walnut, maple, northern red oak, and white oak. Hardwoods come from slow-growing deciduous trees (trees that lose their leaves in winter); they are expensive and generally quite strong. Many hardwoods have beautiful grain patterns and are well suited to woodworking. But they are only used in the most expensive timber-frame construction.

Softwoods come from fast-growing, cone-bearing trees called conifers, or evergreens. Usually much less expensive than hardwoods and widely available at lumberyards, softwoods account for nearly all the lumber used in framing and construction. Though hardwoods are normally stronger because they're more dense, softwoods are certainly more than strong enough for utility framing.

Douglas fir, hemlock, eastern white pine, southern yellow pine, and spruce are all softwoods commonly used for framing. Douglas fir is used for most rough construction, especially along the Pacific Coast, where it is milled. In the South and East you're more likely to find southern pine. There are two other softwoods you might see, redwood and western red cedar, which aren't normally used for framing because of their expense. These species are excellent for exterior siding, trim, and decks because of their exceptional durability and natural resistance to decay.

Sawmills cut softwoods into standard dimensions and lengths. That's why the lumber is sometimes called dimension lumber. Unlike ordering hardwood, ordering softwood framing lumber generally doesn't require that you ask for a specific species of wood. You simply order by dimension and grade. The lumberyard has already made a softwood choice for you by buying whatever wood is available for your region. The lumber is often simply stamped SPF for spruce, pine, fir; it can be any one of these softwood species. To understand lumber and how to use it properly, you need to know about the properties of a tree and the milling process.

Sapwood & Heartwood

There are two kinds of wood in all trees: sapwood and heartwood. Sapwood, as its name implies, carries sap to the leaves. The heartwood is the dense center of the tree. Trees that grow quickly (softwoods) tend to have disproportionately more sapwood. In fact, young trees consist of almost all sapwood. This is important to know when you buy lumber because sapwood and heartwood function differently in buildings. Heartwood, for instance, is used in exposed conditions or for special structural members because it is stronger and more durable. Sapwood is better suited for use as planks, siding, wall studs, and most other building components. And unless it's treated, sapwood lumber is more susceptible to decay than heartwood lumber.

Milled Dimensions

A piece of lumber has two sizes: nominal and actual. A 2x4 may start out at 2x4 inches (its nominal size) when it comes off a log, but it soon shrinks when it is dried. Then it shrinks again when it is planed. A 2x4 soon becomes

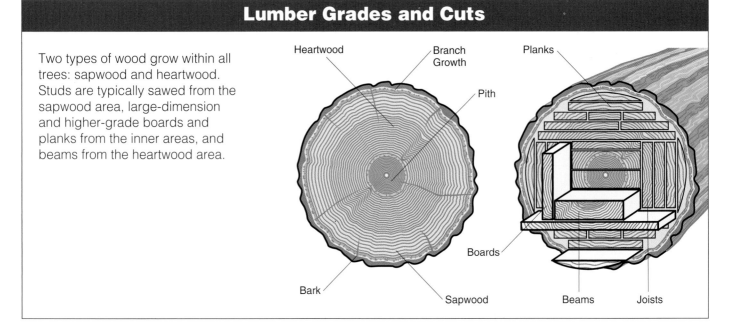

Lumber Grades and Cuts

Two types of wood grow within all trees: sapwood and heartwood. Studs are typically sawed from the sapwood area, large-dimension and higher-grade boards and planks from the inner areas, and beams from the heartwood area.

Heartwood
Branch Growth
Planks
Pith
Boards
Bark
Sapwood
Beams
Joists

1½ x 3½ inches—the lumber's actual size. For wood lengths, the nominal and actual lengths are almost always the same. When you buy a 10-foot 2x4, it is usually 10 feet long (plus an inch or two).

Some lumberyards charge for lumber by the board foot, though increasingly yards are charging by the individual stick, or piece of lumber. If your lumberyard charges you by the board foot, here's how to figure it: take the nominal thickness, multiply it by the nominal width and the length, and divide by 12. A 10-foot 2x6 (usually written 2x6x10' in the industry) would be 10 board feet.

Grades

Besides sapwood and heartwood distinctions, many other wood features come into play, including moisture content, strength, number of knots, and appearance. A standardized system of grading rates wood for many of these qualities. The lower the grade, the poorer the quality.

Lumber grading for structural-grade lumber is complex, with categories, grades, and subgrades. For most framing, you'll find four lumber categories: select structural, No. 1, No. 2, and No. 3. The higher the number, the weaker the wood; the weaker the wood, the less distance you can span. A 2x8 hemlock-fir marked select-structural used as a joist and framed 16 inches on center might span 14 feet 2 inches, for instance, but a No. 3 grade only 11 feet. The wood gets weaker because there are more knots and less consistent grain as you move away from the select-structural grade. You also pay more for stronger wood. For structural framing—joists, rafters, ridge boards—the typical lumber grade is No. 2.

When evaluating 2x4s, you'll find that there are three other names for the No. 1, No. 2, and No. 3 categories.

Construction grade corresponds to No. 1; Standard-Better to No. 2; and Utility to No. 3. (A final category, Economy, is for nonstructural use.) For wall framing, use No. 2 (Standard or Better) for load-bearing and most other walls. Many yards don't stock weaker No. 3 (Utility). Because it's hard to sort this all out, and using utility lumber yields only marginal savings, you can safely buy No. 2 lumber and use it for your entire project.

All lumber has a high moisture content when it is milled. So it is either air-dried or kiln-dried for construction use. The acceptable maximum moisture content for framing wood at a lumberyard is 19 percent. Often the grade stamp for construction lumber will say "KD-19" (kiln-dried 19 percent).

Rough-Sawn Native Green Lumber

Available from some local sawmills, native green lumber's moisture content is usually high because it's sold unseasoned. Also, it's not cut as precisely as standard lumber. A 2x8 can be 2¼ x 8½ inches, for instance, or 2 x 7¼ inches. It's unpredictable. Additionally, native green lumber is not as structurally stable as kiln-dried or air-dried dimension lumber. The wood is heavy and hard to work with, and it cracks and splits as it dries. Native green lumber is inexpensive, however, and it is often used to frame rough structures such as sheds or barns. Also, you can nail it in place soaking wet when you use it for board-and-batten siding.

Pressure-Treated Lumber

Pressure-treated (PT) wood is lumber that's been soaked under pressure with an insecticide and a fungicide, which ward off pests and decay, respectively. It's intended for use anywhere the wood contacts the ground (decks and piers), experiences sustained moisture levels (sills, outdoor stairs), or is subject to insect infestation (any exposed part of your structure in termite areas). PT lumber is mostly southern yellow pine, although some other pines, firs, and hemlocks are used occasionally.

In the past, the most common kind of PT wood was treated with chromated copper arsenate (CCA), a compound that chemically bonds with the wood. CCA-treated lumber has a green tint from the oxidation of the copper. The retention level achieved during treatment determined its use.

Nominal & Actual Lumber Sizes

Nominal Size (in.)	Actual Size (in.)	Nominal Size (in.)	Actual Size (in.)
1x2	¾ x 1½	2x2	1½ x 1½
1x4	¾ x 3½	2x4	1½ x 3½
1x6	¾ x 5½	2x6	1½ x 5½
1x8	¾ x 7¼	2x8	1½ x 7¼
1x10	¾ x 9¼	2x10	1½ x 9¼
1x12	¾ x 11¼	2x12	1½ x 11¼
⁵⁄₄x2	1 x 1½	4x4	3½ x 3½
⁵⁄₄x4	1 x 3½	6x6	5½ x 5½

CCA (and to some extent, all chemical treatments) is controversial: some studies have shown that the arsenic in it dissolves back into the environment under certain circumstances. Manufacturers of these products have voluntarily withdrawn most CCA-treated lumber from the residential market. To fill the void, manufacturers have replaced CCA products with those treated with non-arsenic copper compounds. Most companies have proprietary formulas and market the products under different brand names.

Cautions. Check product data sheets for proper uses of the new treated lumber. One difference you will notice right away is that the signature green tint of CCA-treated lumber is replaced by a brown color that eventually weathers to a gray color as the wood is exposed to the elements.

The other major difference is that there is some evidence that the chemicals used to treat lumber are more corrosive than CCA. This could be a problem with some types of fasteners. Again, check with the manufacturer about fastener selection. Some studies have shown that stainless-steel fasteners offer the best resistance to corrosion. A second choice may be nails and screws finished with a polymer coating.

Rough-sawn green lumber can be ordered from some lumberyards and sawmills. It is beefier (a 2x4 being much closer to 2 in. thick), rougher, and more irregular than finished lumber.

SMART TIP

There are a number of compounds used to treat wood. Be sure the wood you buy is rated for the use you intend, especially lumber that will come in contact with the ground.

Grade Stamps

A typical grade stamp identifies the mill, the grading service's name, the moisture content, the grade, and the species.

The mill identification number isn't really important. The same with the grading service. The species mark is mostly a curiosity, too. But look closely at the biggest word in the grading stamp. You should see a word like STAND, which stands for Standard, the grade you'll use for standard residential-grade light framing. Next, look at the moisture designation. Here's where you'll see KD for kiln-dried, S-DRY, MC, or S-GRN. These are the moisture content ratings mentioned in the "Grades," page 17.

But no matter how much you know, the lumberyard will have already made most framing lumber choices for you, at least in terms of species. You'll simply specify the grade. Check the grading stamp at the yard to make sure you've picked up the right kind of wood.

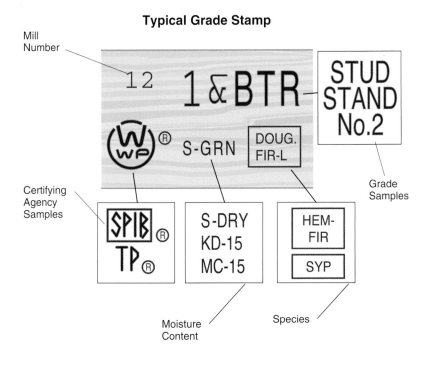

Typical Grade Stamp

Mill Number

12   1&BTR

Certifying Agency Samples

S-GRN   DOUG. FIR-L

STUD STAND No.2

Grade Samples

SPIB TP

S-DRY KD-15 MC-15

HEM-FIR
SYP

Moisture Content

Species

As with any organic material that gains and loses water, wood swells when it is moist and shrinks as it dries. This can lead to warping (uneven shrinking during drying), checking (cracks along growth rings), bowing (end-to-end deviation from the plane of the board's wide face), twisting (spiral or torsional distortion), and cupping (deviation from a flat plane, edge to edge). Softwoods like pine, Douglas fir, and cedar are particularly vulnerable.

Given the demand on the nation's forests for wood, many lumber companies have shortened their harvesting cycles or have planted fast-growing trees. When these trees are harvested, they yield juvenile wood, which can give you problems. Juvenile wood encompasses the first 5 to 20 annual growth rings of any tree, and when it's used for lumber, it doesn't have the same strength as mature wood. You may get bouncy floors, buckled walls, weakened joints, and poorly fitting windows and doors. Even kiln-dried juvenile wood can warp because of nonuniform growth-ring distribution. Inspect the lumber you're buying, and look for telltale signs of juvenile wood, such as uneven grain distribution and warping, and refuse wood that is not up to par.

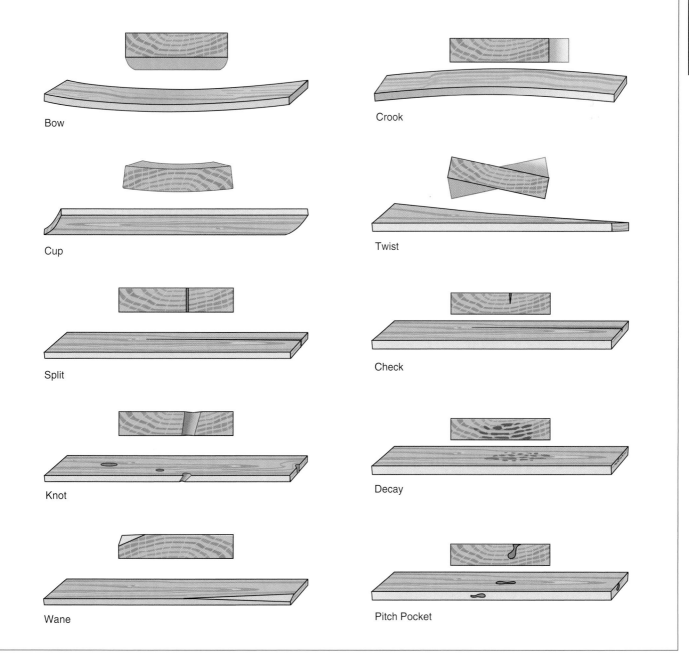

Bow

Crook

Cup

Twist

Split

Check

Knot

Decay

Wane

Pitch Pocket

Plywood & Panel Products

Depending on your design, you might need plywood for floor decking and wall and roof sheathing. Plywood comprises an odd number of thin veneer layers of wood, called plies. The veneers are cross-laminated so the grain of one ply runs perpendicular to another. The veneers are glued and sandwiched together and then heated to over 300°F under 200 pounds per square inch (psi) of pressure. Standard plywood thicknesses are $\frac{5}{16}$, $\frac{3}{8}$, $\frac{7}{16}$, $\frac{15}{32}$, $\frac{1}{2}$, $\frac{5}{8}$, $\frac{23}{32}$, $\frac{3}{4}$, and $1\frac{1}{8}$ inches. If you order $\frac{1}{2}$- and $\frac{3}{4}$-inch plywood for your job, you'll most likely get $\frac{15}{32}$- and $\frac{23}{32}$-inch plywood, respectively. Panels are almost always 4x8 feet after factory trimming. Corner to corner, panels sometimes can be slightly out of square, but not enough to cause problems.

Every piece of plywood has a face veneer and a back veneer. These are the outside plies. The plies under the face and back veneers are called crossbands, and the center ply is called the core. The core can be either veneer or solid lumber. Some plywoods even have fiberglass or particleboard at their cores. Veneer-core plywood is stronger than lumber-core plywood, but lumber-core plywood can hold screws better at its edges.

Used in the right applications, plywood is strong and adds stiffness to walls and strength to floors. Besides conventional sheathing plywood, you can buy treated, fire-retardant, and waterproof plywood for special applications.

Other Panel Products

Panel products other than plywood, called nonveneer or reconstituted wood-product panels, are sometimes used for sheathing. (Check this with your local building department.) Some of these panels are just as strong—and cheaper—than plywood. The products are called reconstituted because they're made from wood particles or wood strands that are bonded together with adhesive into 4x8-foot sheets.

> ## SMART TIP
>
> **Plywood** comes in 4 x 8-foot sheets, but many home centers sell 2 x 4-foot sheets as well. The smaller panels are more expensive per square foot, but they can be handy in a pinch.

Structural Particleboard. Also called flakeboard or chipboard, particleboard is simply a panel of wood particles held together by hot-pressed resin. Some exterior-rated products have a layer of resin or wax on the outside to repel water. The glue used in these products is urea formaldehyde or phenol-formaldehyde adhesive. Some building-code organizations allow you to use structural particleboard as an underlayment or a subfloor. Be sure to check with your code officials.

Oriented-StrandBoard. Usually called OSB, this product also uses strands of wood, but the layers are crossed so that the direction of the grain of each layer is at 90 degrees to the previous layer, just as plywood is cross-laminated to give it strength. The three to five layers of strands in OSB are bonded together with phenolic resin. These panels have a smooth face and are often rated for structural applications. Waferboard, sometimes called strand board, is a similar product, but without the alternating layers of OSB.

Composite Board. Basically a hybrid of plywood and particleboard, composite board has a reconstituted-wood-particle center but a face and back of plywood veneer.

Common Wood Panel Products

Plywood consists of several thin layers glued together with their grains running in alternating directions. Plywood comes in several thicknesses, grades, and ratings that indicate their use.

Structural particleboard is made from wood chips and sawdust glued together typically with urea formaldehyde resin into 4 x 8-ft. sheets. Its uses are often restricted by local building codes.

Oriented-strand board (OSB) is made from opposingly placed strips of scrap wood held together by adhesives under pressure. Some codes allow it for use as sheathing and subflooring.

Rating Panel Products

When you purchase structural panels, a grading label tells you what you're buying. The leading grading association is the APA, The Engineered Wood Association, and you're most likely to see its stamp on panels.

Panel Grade. Panel products are rated in a number of categories. If you look at a typical APA grade stamp, you'll see the panel grade on the top line. This entry designates the proper application for the panel—rated sheathing, rated flooring, rated underlayment, and the like.

Span Rating. Next you'll see a large number or numbers, indicating the span rating. This rating is the recommended center-to-center spacing in inches of studs/joists/rafters over which you can place the panel. If you see numbers like 32/16, the left number shows the maximum spacing in inches of the panel when used in roofing—32 inches of allowable span with three or more supports—and the right number gives the maximum spacing when the panel is used as subflooring—16 inches of allowable span with three or more supports.

Thickness. The grade stamp also identifies the thickness of the panel— $\frac{3}{8}$ inch, $\frac{7}{16}$ inch, $\frac{15}{32}$ inch, $\frac{23}{32}$ inch, and so on.

Exposure. The stamp also lists the exposure and durability classification for plywood. Exterior indicates exposure to weather is possible; Exposure 1 designates suitability for wall and roof sheathing; Exposure 2, for applications that will have low moisture exposure, such as subfloors.

Mill & Standards Numbers. The mill number simply identifies the manufacturer. The remaining numbers on the label—the national evaluation report (NER) and performance-rated panel standard (PRP)—indicate that the panel meets all construction requirements and requisite codes.

Veneer Grades. Plywood is also rated for veneer grades, and that rating appears on the edge of the plywood in combinations of letters. There are six categories in veneer ratings: N, A, B, C Plugged, C, and D, indicating descending order of quality. N is a smooth surface of select woods with no defects, but you won't be using N in framing. It's for use in cabinetry. For construction-grade plywood, the face-and-back-veneer grades are combinations of letters. B-C, for example, is suitable for sheathing, while you'd use A-B when both the face and back veneers will show. A-C or A-D is suitable when only the A side will show.

Common Plywood Types

For most outbuilding projects you'll be using $\frac{1}{2}$-inch or $\frac{5}{8}$-inch BC or CDX plywood—Exposure 1 for wall and roof sheathing and Exposure 2 for subfloors. If you're finishing a barn or shed with plywood alone, you may want to consider AC, which has one "good" side without any repair plugs or major defects.

Another alternative is Texture 1-11, which has grooves cut into it to resemble board siding. T1-11 comes in 4x8-foot and larger panels. Stacking panels produces a seam that should be covered.

1 Tools & Materials

Typical Plywood Grade Stamp

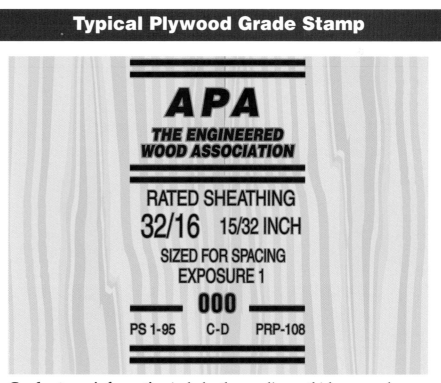

Grade stamp information includes the panel's use, thickness, grade, exposure rating, and mill identification.

Fasteners

Nails

The trick to choosing nails is to match the nail to the task. Codes often specify sizes of common nails for framing because they have an extra-thick shank and a broad head. You should use duplex, or double-headed, nails when you know you'll be removing the nail—in temporary sheathing, for example. Duplex nails allow you to snug the bottom nailhead up tight, but still give your hammer claw purchase to pull them out easily. These types of nails are frequently used for building forms for concrete that will be removed once the material cures.

Besides common nails, you're likely to use ring-shank nails for subflooring; roofing nails and staples for applying felt paper, roofing shingles, and air-infiltration barriers (housewrap); and finishing nails for window- and door-jamb installations. Ring-shank nails have ridges on their shafts for extra holding power. Roofing nails have large heads to hold paper securely. Finishing nails are thin, with small heads that you can easily drive beneath the surface of the wood with a nail set.

Nail Types

Roofing Nail

Box Nail

Finishing Nail

Ring-Shank Nail

Flooring Nail

Drywall Nail

Common Nail

Duplex Nail

Tips on Materials, Delivery, and Storage

Stage deliveries so that your materials aren't back-logged and you'll never run short of what you need. A good approach is to produce all your cut lists at the beginning of the job, break them down into work stages (foundation, rough framing, rafters, sheathing, roofing, windows and doors, siding and interior finish), and assign delivery dates for the materials needed for each work stage.

Using your site plan, with a clear outline of the footprint of your shed, designate some material drops. Lumber is heavy, so have it dropped close by. If you use trusses, which are fragile until set in place, don't schedule delivery until your truss crew is on hand. Windows and doors can go into a near-by garage. Trim lumber or siding should be set in a clean, dry area up on blocks.

Though it may be sunny and dry when materials are delivered, you should protect your deliveries against the elements. Many lumberyards have pallets that they will offer for free to keep the wood off the ground. Covering it with plastic is a good idea, but leave the ends of the wood open to breathe.

Finally, plan your deliveries to take advantage of any labor-saving tools the lumberyards offer. If the delivery truck has a lift, have them place lumber as close to the work site as possible.

Screws

There are many types of screws, but you'll probably use only a few in a shed project: wood screws or deck (bugle-head) screws for joining lumber, and lag screws for making heavy-duty wood-to-wood attachments. Lag screws, sometimes called lag bolts because of their bolt-like heads, are heavy-duty screws that you drive with a socket wrench. They have wide threads for biting into wood like a screw but a hex-shaped head like a bolt. Lag screws are sized according to the diameter of their shanks: usually $5/16$, $3/8$, or $1/2$ inch.

Screw Types

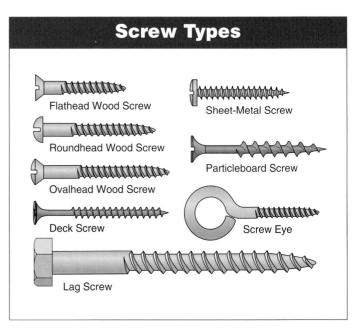

Flathead Wood Screw

Sheet-Metal Screw

Roundhead Wood Screw

Particleboard Screw

Ovalhead Wood Screw

Deck Screw

Screw Eye

Lag Screw

Nail Sizes and Weights

Pennyweight	Length (in.)	Nails/lb. (Common)
2d	1	876
3d	1¼	568
4d	1½	316
5d	1¾	271
6d	2	181
7d	2¼	161
8d	2½	106
10d	3	69
12d	3¼	63
16d	3½	49
20d	4	31
30d	4½	24
40d	5	18
60d	6	14

SMART TIP

Once the shed is complete, go over the area around the structure with a magnet to pick up any nails or screws dropped during construction, especially if children will be playing around the shed or if you park your car in the area. Heavy duty magnets can be rented by the day from tool-supply sources, including some home centers.

Bolts

Bolts fall into three main categories: carriage bolts, machine bolts, and stove bolts. Specialty bolts add many more categories to the list and ones designed for specific functions. There are also about a dozen kinds of nuts and at least four kinds of washers. Each category of bolt, nut, and washer has a specific type of use.

You probably won't find many framing applications for machine bolts, which have hex- or square-shaped heads, and stove bolts, which have rounded heads with a slot for a screwdriver. But carriage bolts, which have unslotted oval heads, can be effective when attaching structural lumber face-to-face or major timbers to posts. Carriage bolts have a square shoulder just beneath the head that digs into the wood as you tighten the bolt, which prevents it from slipping and spinning in the hole, and they are sized according to the diameter of their shanks and their length.

Another bolt you're likely to use, the anchor bolt, attaches the sill plate to the top of a foundation of large sheds. Wedge-type bolts and J-bolts are the most common types.

Wood and deck screws are generally slotted or Phillips head, although there are others available. These screws are sized by their thickness, referred to by number. A screw's number indicates the diameter of its shank, the solid shaft of the screw measured at the base of the threads near the head. Common sizes are #6, #8, and #10. Of course, lengths can vary. A #8 screw, for example, can be nearly any length up to about 3½ inches. The heavier the gauge, the more likely you are to find it in longer lengths.

Screw Sizes

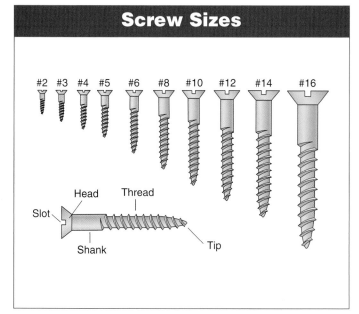

Bolt Types

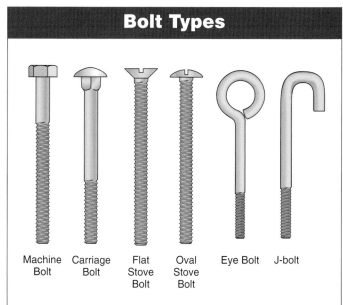

chapter 2
foundations

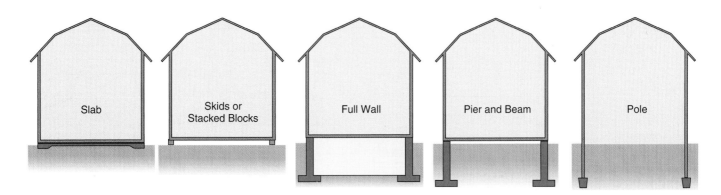

Slab | Skids or Stacked Blocks | Full Wall | Pier and Beam | Pole

Types of Foundations

Most sheds will not need a permanent foundation like the one you have on your house. In most cases, the foundations used on the three sheds we built for this book will serve adequately. Two of our sheds were constructed on stacked blocks, and one was built on pressure-treated timbers. But regulations in your area may require a more permanent foundation, so check with the building department.

Building Foundations

There are a variety of foundation types from which to choose. For example, if you're building on heavy clay soil, a shed built on skids may make the job easier. A shed that requires a more stable foundation may require a concrete slab with footings.

The way you plan on using your new shed can determine which type of foundation is best. If you are going to use your shed for storing garden tools, blocks stacked on gravel pads will suffice. If the shed will be a workshop of some type, you may want a slab foundation. Or you may want to support the shed with poured concrete piers.

Lay Out the Foundation

To lay out the rough corners of a basic building, you'll need four 2x4 stakes and a measuring tape. To find the location of your building's corners, measure from your property line or from an existing structure on your property. To make sure your layout is square, measure the diagonals (they will be the same length in a square or rectangle), or use the 3-4-5 triangulation method, below. To lay out large foundations, especially those being built on a slope, it's wise to use a transit level or builder's level.

If you're not going to excavate the area using heavy machinery, you can tie mason's string to nails on the corner boards and keep these lines as your layout marks. Once the layout is square, if the strings will get in your way, use spray paint to mark the ground beneath the lines. If you need to excavate the site with heavy equipment, however, you'll need to build batter boards, which move the stakes outside of the building layout. (See "Making Batter Boards," page 26.) Otherwise, a bulldozer or backhoe will destroy your corner boards.

Squaring Corners

Check to make sure corners of the foundation layout are square by using the 3-4-5 method of triangulation. Starting at corner A, measure 3 feet along one guideline, and mark point B. Starting again from corner A, measure 4 feet along the guideline perpendicular to the first one, and mark point C. Adjust the AC line until the distance BC is exactly 5 feet. Angle BAC is now a true 90-degree angle. You can double-check the squareness of corners and the overall layout by measuring the diagonals between opposite corners.

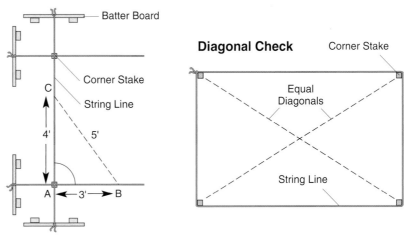

3-4-5 Triangulation

Batter Board
Corner Stake
String Line
C
4'
5'
A ← 3' → B

Diagonal Check

Corner Stake
Equal Diagonals
String Line

Making Batter Boards

1. Cut 16 stakes (four for each corner) from 2x4s, about 3 ft. long, with pointed ends. These stakes support the horizontal batter boards.

2. Set pairs of 2x4 stakes at roughly right angles to each other, 2 ft. or more outside the corners and parallel with the lines of the foundation.

3. Make batter boards by cutting 2-ft. 1x4s. After drilling pilot holes, screw the batter boards to the stakes, using clamps to hold the boards in position.

4. Use a level to check the batter boards. This allows you to stretch level string lines along the perimeter of the building foundation.

5. Tack nails into the batter boards. Then fasten guidelines to the nails in the boards to establish the exact building corners and overall outline.

Block Foundations

A block foundation consists of blocks stacked on a base of ¾-inch gravel. Ideally, the gravel should extend below the frost line, especially in areas that are subject to frost heave. This type of foundation keeps excavation at a minimum. Simply dig a hole that accommodates the dimensions of the block plus a 6-inch border around the block. In most cases, a 4 to 6-foot spacing will suffice, but check requirements with your local building inspector.

With this type of foundation, it is the weight of the shed itself that holds the structure in place. However, many local codes now require steel anchors on sheds to prevent the shed from blowing over during periods of high winds. These anchors are driven through the shed's floor framing and into the ground.

Another option is to build a concrete footing and attach blocks to the footing with mortar. To attach the blocks to the framing of the shed, fill the hollow block with concrete, and install anchor bolts in the concrete before it sets.

Anchor bolts are set into the top course of block or into concrete. With a framing square, measure from the outside edge of the block or slab to the bolt; then mark that distance in from the sill's edge.

Solid concrete blocks provide a good foundation for most garden sheds. For hilly sites, use the blocks to create a level base for the floor. A bead of construction adhesive will hold the stack in place.

Building a Skid Foundation

Rot-resistant timber skids made of pressure-treated lumber can ably serve as a shed foundation. The timbers you select should be rated for ground contact. To facilitate drainage, the timbers should sit on a bed of ¾-inch gravel that is at least 6 inches deep. However, some building departments may require a deeper bed of gravel, especially in areas subject to frost heave.

The gravel bed under the timbers has to extend under all of the timbers used. Excavating this large area by hand can be a real chore. Consider hiring a landscaper to excavate the area and fill it to grade with gravel.

1 After laying out the outline of your shed on the ground, use a shovel to excavate out the first 4 or 5 in. of soil. Tamp the remaining subgrade firm with a hand tamper or the end of a 2x4.

2 Cover the hole with landscape fabric or 6-mil perforated polyethylene sheeting, and fill it in with gravel. This will help the drainage and keep the foundation timbers from rotting.

3 Place two 4x4 or 6x6 timbers, pressure-treated and rated for ground contact, parallel with each other. Align their outer edges with the outer edges of the shed.

4 Check the timbers for level, and add or subtract gravel as needed. Use a straight 2x4 longer than the width of the shed to make sure that the timbers are level with each other.

Working with Concrete

Concrete is a mixture of portland cement, sand, gravel, and water. You can purchase the dry ingredients separately or buy them premixed, generally in 80-pound bags.

Mixing Options

For large-scale projects, however, you should order ready-mix concrete. It is sold by the cubic yard and delivered in a truck ready to pour. For smaller jobs—for example, form-tube piers for a small storage shed—you can mix your own concrete by adding water according to the instructions of the bag or by following the table, "Concrete Ingredients by Proportion," opposite.

But don't get too ambitious. One cubic yard, only enough for an 8x10-foot 4-inch slab, would require about 40 of those 80-pound bags. For mid-size jobs or those that a concrete truck can't drive to, it makes sense to rent a portable power mixer. For estimating purposes, you can make about 1 cubic yard of concrete with five 94-pound bags of portland cement, 14 cubic feet of sand, and 21 cubic feet of gravel.

Mixing Concrete

1 If concrete is too wet, ridges made in the mix with a trowel won't hold their shape. The concrete will be easy to mix and pour, but will not settle evenly nor provide its rated strength.

2 If concrete is too dry, you won't be able to make any ridges in the mix. It will be difficult to work. Mainly, the concrete will not cure properly and will not develop required strength.

3 When the concrete is mixed correctly, the ridges will hold most of their shape; only a little water will be visible on the surface. Place the concrete before it becomes too stiff.

Curing Concrete

1 To keep concrete sufficiently moist during the curing process, you can periodically spray the finished surface lightly but thoroughly with water from a garden hose.

2 A chemical curing compound, applied to concrete with a paint roller or air-powered paint sprayer, is one way to prevent water loss during curing. Apply it after the surface has set up.

3 Another way to prevent concrete from drying prematurely is to cover the slab with plastic sheeting. Burlap or straw can also be used but must be kept moist.

Ordering Concrete

Before you call, have an estimate for your order. Most ready-mix contractors will require only a day's notice. It's important to double-check your measurements of length times width times depth (and your calculations) to specify the order in cubic yards. Always round up your numbers so that you don't run short of material.

Mix Variations

When hand-mixing, you may be tempted to adjust the mix proportions—say, by adding more water to make the concrete easier to mix and pour. However, as water content can drastically affect strength, the best policy is to order ready-mixed concrete or precisely follow directions on the bags.

The standard proportion of water to cement produces concrete with a compressive strength of 3,000 to 4,000 pounds per square inch (psi). Adding less water makes mixing more difficult and could weaken the mix.

Ready-mix concrete is also available with additives unavailable to the DIYer. One type produces microscopic air bubbles. This air-entrained concrete is more resistant to cracking than concrete you mix on site. There are also additives that accelerate the curing time for concrete poured in cold weather. You can order ready-mix concrete to a greater compressive strength than hand-mixed concrete, to support a greater building load.

Curing

The process of hardening concrete and bringing it to its full strength is called curing. Concrete begins to harden as soon as it is mixed and can support your weight within a few hours. Most of the curing takes place in the first two weeks, but it takes a month to reach near its peak hardness. The thicker the concrete, the more time it needs to cure completely. Most concrete needs to be kept moist over seven consecutive days above 50° F to cure properly. If the temperature is above 70° F, the concrete may cure in five days; highly-early-strength concrete needs only three. Curing concrete can be sprinkled periodically with water and covered with plastic sheeting, burlap, canvas, or straw to limit dehydration. There are also liquid curing compounds that you can roll onto concrete.

Curing in Extreme Heat. Concrete will dehydrate too quickly in hot weather, robbing it of the water it needs to cure. In extreme cases, a steady hot, dry breeze can accelerate evaporation so that the surface begins to set before it can be smoothed. There are some solutions, such as adding flaked ice or cooling down the aggregates with a sprinkler before adding them to the mix. To eliminate the risk of wasting your efforts on a job that is not going to last, don't pour in temperatures over 90°F. It's also important to remember that if the mix makes contact with a hot surface, moisture may burn off immediately. It's wise to spray some cool water on forms that are sitting in the sun as well as on the reinforcing bar, which can get quite hot to the touch.

Concrete Ingredients by Proportion

| Maximum Size | Air-Entrained Concrete | | | | Concrete without Air | | | |
| | Number of Parts per Ingredient | | | | Number of Parts per Ingredient | | | |
Course Aggregate Inches	Cement	Sand*	Coarse Aggregate	Water	Cement	Sand*	Coarse Aggregate	Water
⅜	1	2¼	1½	½	1	2½	1½	½
½	1	2¼	2	½	1	2½	2	½
¾	1	2¼	2½	½	1	2½	2½	½
1	1	2¼	2¾	½	1	2½	2¾	½
1½	1	2¼	3	½	1	2½	3	½

Note: 7.48 gallons of water equals 1 cubic foot. One 94-pound bag of portland cement equals about 1 cubic foot.
*"Wet" sand sold for most construction use.
The combined finished volume is approximately two-thirds the sum of the bulk volumes.

Piers and Posts

Concrete piers should be set into the ground every 6 to 8 feet under your shed. The shed's floor joists are attached to the piers with fasteners. This provides strong anchor points that tie the shed to the ground. Excavating for circular piers (which are often created by remain-in-place fiber forms) can be done by hand with a posthole digger. It's hard work, but you can rent a gas-powered posthole digger called a power auger. Note that gas-powered augers are hard to control (especially on sloped sites), and they take a great deal of strength to position and operate.

Piers can also be created by using the ground itself serving as a form; these are called "formless piers," but they do not work well in areas where there is sandy soil or heavy frost heaving. The bottom photo sequence provides step-by-step information on how to create formless piers.

SMART TIP

To manage piles of gravel, spread out sheets of 6-mil polyethylene on the lawn, and dump the gravel on the sheets. The material won't migrate into the lawn and cleanup will go faster.

Setting Piers with Form Tubes

1 Dig holes for your piers with a posthole digger or power auger to below the frost depth. Rocky or wooded soil will be difficult to work. Fill the bottom with 2 in. of gravel for support and drainage.

2 Insert a fiber form tube into the hole. It should protrude from the soil level about 6 in. Cut off any excess with a handsaw. Plumb the inside of the form with a spirit level to ensure straightness.

Setting Formless Piers

1 Use a shovel and a posthole digger—or to save time, a rented power auger—to excavate a hole for a formless pier. The earthen walls of the hole serve as the formwork.

2 Measure the depth of the hole carefully to make sure that the base of the pier will rest on undisturbed or compacted soil that is below the minimum frost depth for your region.

3 Check the form tube for plumb and level. Then backfill around the form with soil. Remove large rocks from the fill; small rocks can be added near the bottom of the hole.

4 Pour concrete from a wheelbarrow directly into the form. Before the concrete hardens, insert a J-bolt into the center, leaving the threads above the concrete surface.

5 After the concrete sets, attach post-base hardware using a washer and nuts. The post sits on a metal standoff that allows for drainage and keeps the bottom of the post dry.

3 The bottom of the hole should be tamped down with a tamper or the end of a 2x4 or 4x4. Fill the hole with the required concrete mix and steel reinforcement bars.

4 Insert a metal base for a post or girder into the concrete when the mix is just firm enough to hold it but not yet hardened. The base keeps the bottom of the post from coming in contact with the ground.

5 Adjust the hardware so that it is level, plumb, and properly oriented to support the structural post or beam, which will be installed later. Once the concrete has set, it can't be adjusted.

Concrete Footings

For larger structures and in areas subject to frost heave, footings are the first step to a complete perimeter wall foundation or floor slab. (Some slabs are monolithic, which means that both footing and slab are poured at once.)

Assembling the Forms

Using your batter boards and strings as guides, dig the footing to the required width and depth. In some cases, part of the footing may extend above grade. If the soil is loose at the bottom of the trench, compact it with a tamper to prevent the concrete from settling. If you remove large rocks, fill the depressions and tamp them down firmly.

Drive stakes for the forms 18 to 24 inches apart. Clamp on the form boards before fastening them. Attach 1x2 braces across the top of the forms every 2 feet or so to keep them from spreading when you pour the concrete. To keep cracks from forming, place steel reinforcing bars (#4 rebar) horizontally. You may need several rows for deep footings. Before you pour the concrete, double-check to make sure the form boards are level and plumb.

Pouring the Concrete

Pour or shovel wet concrete into the forms, flush to the top. As you pour, use a shovel or mason's hoe to work out any air pockets. Use a wood float, flat trowel, or short length of 2x4 to smooth the top surface of the footing. After smoothing and leveling the concrete, set anchor bolts into the concrete 1 foot from the ends of each wall and 6 feet on center. The bolts are used to secure the sill plate that anchors the structure to the foundation. If the footing will support a block wall, you'll need to add vertical rebars to tie the wall to the footing.

SMART TIP

Before pouring the concrete, double-check with the local building department that your shed meets any setback requirements that may apply and that the footing reaches the proper depth for your area. Protect your lawn from the wheels of your wheelbarrow by laying a path made of wide planks from your driveway to the shed building site.

Building Footing Forms

1. After setting up batter boards and marking the perimeter, begin excavating the soil within your string lines. Remember, the footings must reach below the local frost-depth line.

2. Drive in the stakes to support the form boards. You can build them from 1x4s or 2x4s with an angle cut to form the tip. Most footings are twice the width of the wall.

3. Use a clamp to fasten the form boards to the stakes temporarily. Check the boards for level; adjust them as needed; and then nail or screw the boards to the stakes.

4. Secure any butt joints in the formwork with ½-in.-thick plywood gussets. Use a power drill and 1½-in. screws to fasten these in place across the exterior face of each joint.

5. Use 1x2 spreaders to bridge the forms every few feet. These braces ensure that the weight of the concrete as it is poured will not cause the forms to bulge.

1 Support rebar at the proper height at least an inch or two off the ground with pieces of brick. Wire supports called chairs work better than bricks if you can find them.

2 Secure the rebar to the chairs or supports with wire ties, twisted tightly with pliers. This keeps the supports from being forced out of position by the concrete during the pour.

3 You'll need to bend the rebar around corners. Adjoining pieces of rebar should be lapped by several inches to provide unbroken support. Secure the laps together with wire ties.

4 Transport the concrete to the formwork. Use a shovel to distribute the concrete evenly, filling the forms completely (left). Tamp the concrete in order to eliminate voids or air bubbles, especially in corners (right).

5 Once the footing has cured, use a mason's trowel to fill corners, working along the inside edges of the form boards.

6 Use a 2x4 screed board to fill the forms evenly and strike off excess concrete (left). Embed steel anchor bolts (for sills) or rebar (for block walls) into the concrete at 6 ft. on center and within 1 ft. of each corner or door opening (right).

Concrete Slabs

The concrete slab, often called a slab-on-grade (the grade being the surface of the ground), is a monolithic piece of concrete, usually 4 to 6 inches thick, poured onto the ground over a bed of gravel within forms. Local codes specify the thickness of slabs for different purposes.

Soil preparation beneath a slab is crucial. Before you form a slab, prepare the soil to ensure proper drainage around and beneath it. In cold climates, this might mean replacing the soil to 50 percent of the frost depth with gravel. In some parts of the country, a polyethylene vapor barrier should be placed between the soil and the gravel base.

Formwork

Around the edges, a slab is formed by boards: 2x6s, 2x8s, 2x10s, 2x12s, or a combination of these. Use 2x4 scab boards to hold the form boards together as you place them around the perimeter. Be careful to keep them plumb: check periodically with a spirit level. Brace and stake the boards in place using 2x2s or 2x4s, either driven into the ground or run diagonally as kickers. Also use a water level or transit to check that the forms are level across their tops.

When positioning the slab form boards, use mason's string as a guide. A batter-board system (page 26) for defining form placement works well and provides a precise string outline to follow when forming the slab perimeter.

(page 26)

Reinforcement

You must reinforce concrete slabs with steel rods called rebar and welded-wire mesh. Within footings, you lay #4 rebar, and in the main area of the slab itself use #10 reinforcing mesh. The rebar will also serve as an anchor for the J-bolts, which hold the sill plates in place once the concrete dries and you start framing. (You can also place the J-bolts in the wet concrete.) Most codes call for J-bolts no more than 6 feet apart.

Slab Footings

Most slabs are thicker around their outside perimeters to carry the load of the structure. This thicker section is called the footing. The footing and slab are integrally one piece of concrete, poured at the same time. To create the footing, dig deeper where you want the footing so that more concrete can be poured into the excavation. If you have unstable soil, use 2x8s or 2x10s to form the sides of the footing.

Construction Gravel Basics

Gravel is commonly used beneath foundations, footings, piers, and slabs because it doesn't retain water and therefore helps defeat frost heaving. The most commonly used gravel for this purpose is ¾ gravel ("three-quarter gravel"). This means that the individual stones are a maximum ¾ inch diameter. Gravel is available as small as ¼ inch in diameter.

Other types of construction stone include pea gravel—which is made up of round, smooth stones—and crushed stone, which provides a stable base because the rock surfaces interlock with one another.

Slab Construction

Concrete slabs need to be built on a bed of compacted soil and 4 to 6 in. of gravel. Rebar and welded-wire mesh add strength and tie the thinner slab to the thicker footings.

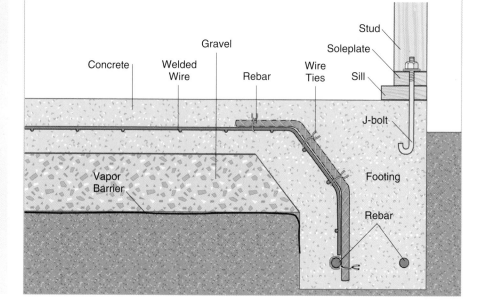

Pouring a Slab

1 To strengthen the concrete, lay welded wire within the slab, generally on short supports called chairs. You can also use bricks or rocks to keep the wire above the soil.

2 If the slab will also be the finished floor, control joints will hide any cracks in the bottom of the joint. They can be formed into the pour or cut with a concrete saw after the slab hardens.

3 After you have evenly distributed the concrete throughout the form, you'll use a screed board to strike off the excess and fill in the hollows. Use a 2x4 slightly longer than the width of the slab.

4 As concrete pours from the ready-mix truck, use hoes and shovels to spread it evenly throughout the slab forms. You'll need many helpers while the mix is still plastic.

5 You can smooth (with a float) the rough surface left by screeding or texture it with a broom.

2 Foundations

Estimating Concrete for Slabs

Square Feet

(chart with axes: Square Feet 300–0 across top; Cubic Feet 0–200 down left; Cubic Yards 0–7 down right; diagonal lines labeled 4" THICK, 5" THICK, 6" THICK, 7" THICK, 8" THICK)

To figure out how much concrete to mix or order, you can use the chart at left. If you prefer, total up the volume inside the forms in cubic feet (length x height x width); then divide this figure by 27 to convert it into the ordering standard of cubic yards. To avoid a shortfall, it's smart to build in a reasonable excess factor of about 8 percent by changing the conversion factor to 25. Remember that an 80-pound bag of concrete mix will make only two-thirds of a cubic foot. Large orders measured in cubic yards will require a rented power mixer (and many bags of premixed concrete) or delivery from a concrete truck.

chapter 3
building basics

Floor Framing

Framing houses and other large structures requires a great deal of specialized information dealing with sizing lumber to account for "live" and "dead loads." The requirements for simple sheds—those in the 8x10-foot-size range—are not as stringent. You will build a sturdy, long-lasting structure if you use 2x6 joists and rafters, and 2x4 studs. In most cases, there is no need to top windows and doors with beefed-up headers, but you should always check with the local building inspector before starting work.

For floors, create a frame the size of the perimeter of the building using joist stock and adding joists every 16 inches on center in the interior of the frame. For most of the sheds in this book, this type of floor simply rests on the foundation blocks. The weight of the structure keeps it in place. However, some municipalities require ground anchors to hold the shed on its foundation. The steel anchors are driven through the framing and into the ground.

Installing Floor Framing

1. Place the rim joists on top of the sill (with both slab and wall foundations) or the beam (on pier foundations for a small shed as shown here).

2. Tack the joists in place, and stop to check the perimeter frame to make sure it's square. Use a framing square at the corners, and measure the overall diagonals, which should be equal.

3. End-nail the rim joists and end joist together with three 16d common nails. Check that they are tight

against the sill. You may want to predrill nailholes near the ends to prevent splitting.

4. Mark your layout on opposite headers using 16-in. on-center marks, depending on the span and load. You may want to make duplicate layouts on both boards before installing them.

5. Once square, you can end-nail the joists through the rim joist using three 12d common nails. Local codes generally require that you set joists into metal joist hangers.

Wall Framing

Stick-built walls are constructed on a modular system designed to provide a combination of structural strength and nailing surfaces for sheathing materials inside and out. Adding windows and doors generally requires extra studs because the openings don't normally fall exactly into the modular plan.

The base of the wall is a horizontal 2x4 (or a 2x6 in some cases) called a soleplate, or shoe. Studs sit on the shoe, generally every 16 inches on center. The top of the wall is capped with two more horizontal 2x4s called a top plate.

There are three kinds of studs in most walls. Full-height studs, sometimes called king studs, run from the soleplate to the top plate. Jack studs, also called trimmer studs, run from the shoe up alongside a full stud at rough openings. The top of the jack stud rests under the header over a window or door. Cripple studs are short 2x4s that fill in the spaces above and below a rough opening—for example, from the soleplate to the sill of a window. They are spaced to maintain the modular layout and provide nailing surfaces for siding and drywall or other surface materials.

Assembling the Wall

Start by marking the plate and shoe according to the wall layout in your plans. Then you can cut the studs. A power miter box makes this job go quickly. King studs will be full length—generally 91½ inches for 8-foot ceilings. Jack studs will be king-stud length minus the combined height of the header and cripples above. You can cut the cripples and sills to length after you put the jack studs and headers in place. Some builders prefer to build rough openings after the wall has been raised.

One efficient way to build walls is to assemble the components on the deck and tip them into position. On long walls you'll need some help raising the structure, and on all walls you have to plan the framing carefully before nailing through the shoe and first plate and into the ends of the studs.

Squaring the Wall

Check walls to make sure they're square before you stand them in place, and again after you raise them. You can check the diagonals, which should be equal if the wall is square. It also helps to lock up the position by tacking diagonal braces along the wall. Some builders also install sheathing before raising, although this makes the wall even heavier.

Wall Framing

A stick-framed wall consists of studs—vertical 2x4s or 2x6s—between a single horizontal soleplate, often called a shoe, and a double top plate. Windows and doors have framed headers and extra jack and cripple studs to account for the missing full studs.

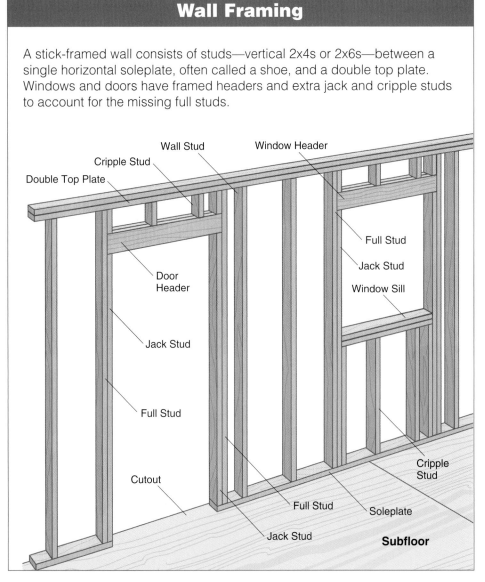

Double Top Plate · Cripple Stud · Wall Stud · Window Header · Door Header · Jack Stud · Full Stud · Cutout · Full Stud · Jack Stud · Full Stud · Soleplate · Full Stud · Jack Stud · Window Sill · Cripple Stud · Subfloor

---

SMART TIP

While they don't provide structural support, cripple studs above and below windows maintain the 16-inch-on-center spacing needed for attaching wall sheathing. When cutting cripple studs, measure the length of the stud carefully and cut one stud. If it fits, use it as a template to cut the others. You will need to take measurements for each window and door.

Raising the Wall

Before erecting any wall, snap a chalk line along the sub-floor or slab to establish a reference guide for positioning the inside edge of the wall soleplate. On a subfloor, also nail a few 2x4 cleats to the outside of the header joist to keep the wall from slipping off the deck as you raise it. With as many helpers as you need, slide the wall into position so that when you raise it, it will stand close to the guideline. Erect the wall, and align it to the chalk line.

Using a 4-foot spirit level, get the wall as close to plumb as possible. You'll fine-tune it for plumb when you install the adjacent wall. Run braces from studs to cleats that are nailed into the subfloor or on corners. (See "Wall Bracing," page 40.) When the wall is plumb, have a helper nail the braces to the cleats. With the bottom sole-plate properly positioned, nail into the rim joists and floor joists using 16d nails. You can plumb a small wall by yourself. The trick is to nail an angled brace to a cleat on

---

Laying Out the Walls

To lay out the soleplate and top plates of a wall, first cut a pair of straight 2x4s (or 2x6s) to length. Tack the soleplate to the subfloor and set the top plate flush against it. Make your first mark ¾ inch short of your on-center spacing (15¼ inches), and make an X past that mark. This will place center of the first stud 16 inches from the corner. Measure down the length of the plates, and mark where the common, full-length studs will fall, every 16 or 24 inches, and mark each of these studs with an X. You can also measure and mark the locations of cripple studs (C) and jack studs (O).

Avoid layout confusion by marking the shoe and the top plate the same way in a step-ahead system. You may want to mark the soleplate and top plate at the same time with a combination square.

Once the square line is drawn, step ahead of the line to mark the location of a stud with an X. You can also use the tongue of a framing square, which is 1½ inches wide, to mark the full width.

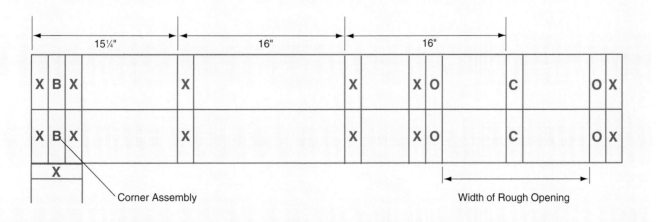

Lay out corners and rough openings on your plates as indicated on your plans. Mark all full-length studs with an X, jack studs (also called trimmers) with an O, blocking with a B, and cripples with a C.

the deck and clamp it to the wall. Check using a level, adjust and reclamp as needed, and tack the brace to hold the wall plumb. On long walls of 20 feet or so, brace each corner and several interior studs.

To check for plumb, hold a 4-foot level against a straight 2x4. Pay particular attention to corners. If the wall is leaning in or out, release any braces and adjust the wall. Apply force to the braces to push the wall out. To bring the wall in, attach a flat brace between two cleats (one attached to the wall and one to the floor) and use a two-by as a kicker to bow the brace and force the wall inward. You can also apply braces staked outside the building. Retack the braces to hold the wall in its proper position.

Top Plates

When adjoining walls are in proper position you can add the second top plate and tie the walls together. The top plate on one wall overlaps the bottom plate of the adjoining wall. Where partitions join exterior bearing walls, the top plate of the partition should lap onto the top plate of the exterior wall. Secure laps using at least two 16d nails.

Wall Bracing

Site-built wall braces come in handy during construction. Use them to hold a wall in place or to force an uneven wall into plumb.

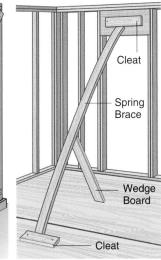

Temporary Corner Brace

Cleat

Spring Brace

Wedge Board

Cleat

To brace a corner, lock it in place using a 2x4. Leave the brace in place until the whole wall is finished—nail it outside the frame so it's out of the way.

Apply a spring brace to fix a bow in a stud wall. Nail a flat brace (at least 8 ft. long) to cleats on the floor and wall, and force the wall into plumb.

Stud Configurations at Corners

If you plan on finishing the interior of your shed, you will need to provide a nailing base at the corners for the finish material, such as drywall or paneling. Stud-and-block corners use the most material, but they are the most rigid. The three-stud corner saves time and a little material because you don't need the blocking. The two-stud corner is fine for a small shed with unfinished interior walls.

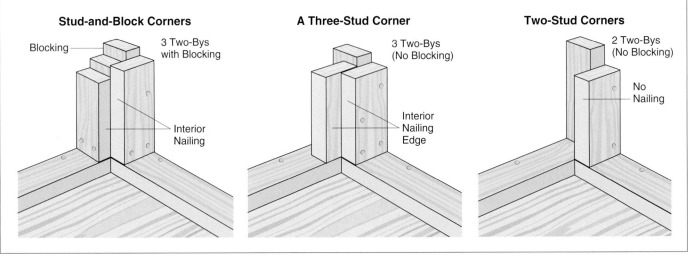

Stud-and-Block Corners
Blocking — 3 Two-Bys with Blocking — Interior Nailing

A Three-Stud Corner
3 Two-Bys (No Blocking) — Interior Nailing Edge

Two-Stud Corners
2 Two-Bys (No Blocking) — No Nailing

Windows & Doors

Stud placement is crucial for rough openings in walls where you insert doors and windows. The rough opening size is listed in window and door catalogs, including about ½ to ¾ inch of shimming space around the unit. This allows you to plumb and level the window or door even when the adjacent wall frame is out of kilter.

Each side of the opening has a full-height stud. Inside that stud is a shorter jack stud. The distance jack to jack, allowing for shimming space, is the rough opening.

On windows, a short jack stud helps to support the sill. You add a jack stud that runs from the sill up to the header. On most sheds, there is no need to install a beefy header above the window as shown below,

simply frame the opening using 2x4s, but check with the building inspector for requirements in your area.

On doors, you need two long jack studs that run from the floor to the header, with cripple studs above. You can rest the jacks on the soleplate, or run them down to the plywood deck. This covers the shoe end grain and on exterior doors will bear on the joist or rim joist below.

Building Rough Openings

1 At each side of the rough opening, nail a jack stud into the soleplate and adjacent full-height stud. In 2x4 walls, use two 10d nails every foot or so for stability.

2 Continue additional jack stud sections along both sides of the window opening. These framing members will help to support the weight carried by the header across the opening.

3 Make up a header with two 2x6s, sandwiching a sheet of ½-in. plywood that packs out the header to the wall thickness. Wider openings may require larger headers.

4 Add cripple studs above the header and below the sill to maintain the on-center layout of the wall. You need the cripples for nailing surfaces (and support) under surface materials.

Framing Roofs

Though this section of the book will provide detailed rafter cutting instructions, along with the basic geometry required for calculating rafter length, you probably won't need all this information. Here's why: in the project sections of this book, we will show how to build sheds that are relatively small. Someone with even limited carpentry experience can easily calculate the angles where the rafter meets the top plate on a wall and the ridgeboard. You can cut and trim just one rafter until it fits snugly, and then use this rafter as a "master" to mark and cut the remaining rafters.

Roofing Measurements

If you know the slope of a roof but don't know the total rise, you can determine that dimension using the total run on a symmetrical roof. First, divide the span in half to get the total run. Let's say your structure has a span of 20 feet. The total run is 10 feet. Now multiply the unit rise by the number of feet in the total run. An 8-in-12 roof with a total run of 10 feet means the total rise is 80 inches (8 x 10), or 6 feet 8 inches. If you increase the run, the slope doesn't change, but the total rise increases. For example, if you have a 12-foot run with an 8-in-12 roof, the total rise is 96 inches (8 x 12), or 8 feet.

When you determine rise, you use a measurement along a line from the cap plate's top outside edge to the ridge's centerline. The point at which the rafter measuring line and the ridgeboard centerline intersect is known as the theoretical ridgeboard height. The rise is the distance from the plate to the theoretical ridgeboard height.

But if math is not your strong point, there is another option. You erect braced posts at each end of the ridge, adjust the ridge up or down as needed using clamps, and test rafters for length, angle, and end cuts. This may be the best system for do-it-yourselfers working on an attached shed and trying to match an existing roof line.

Roof Measurements

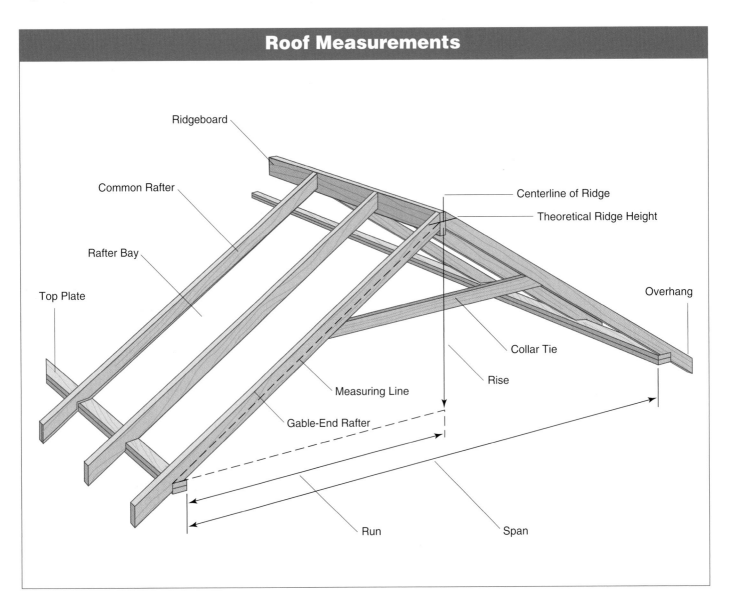

Ridgeboard

Common Rafter

Rafter Bay

Top Plate

Centerline of Ridge

Theoretical Ridge Height

Overhang

Collar Tie

Measuring Line

Rise

Gable-End Rafter

Run

Span

Roof Terminology

Rise is the height of the roof at its ridge measured from the top plate of the end wall below the ridge.

Span is the horizontal distance from wall to wall. A roof's span does not include the overhang at the eaves.

Run is the horizontal distance from one wall to a point under the ridge, or typically half the span.

Pitch is the angle of a roof as a ratio of the rise to the span. A 24-foot-wide structure, for example, with a gable roof that rises 10 feet from side wall to ridgeboard has a pitch of 10/24 or 5/12. A pitch of 1/4 or 1/3 is common for gable roofs. A Cape Cod–style roof might have a 1/2 pitch.

Slope is expressed as the rafter's vertical rise in inches, or unit rise, per 12 inches of horizontal run, or unit run. If a slope has a unit rise of 4 and a unit run of 12, the roof surface rises 4 inches for every 12 inches along the run line. This is expressed as 4:12 or 4 in 12. On most building plans, you'll notice a right triangle off to the side—for example, 4 in 12 with a 12 at the top of the triangle on one leg of the right angle and a 4 on the other leg. The hypotenuse of the triangle shows you the angle of slope. The higher the number of inches in unit rise, the steeper the roof. A 12-in-12 roof, common in Cape Cod-style roofs, rises a foot in elevation for every foot of run (a 45-degree angle).

Roof Trusses

Rather than cutting your own roof rafters, you can use roof trusses. For sheds, trusses are usually 2x4s held together by metal gussets. Order them from a truss manufacturer by specifying the length of the bottom cord, which includes the span of the shed, the thickness of the walls, and the soffits or overhangs if any. The manufacturer will tell you the number you will need for your shed. You will probably need a helper to lift and install the trusses.

Gable Framing

Calculating rafter length and the angles at the ridge and rafter tail is more complex than framing walls. But the job is doable using only basic math if you break down the task into smaller, more simple steps. On gable roofs, you can either run the rafters individually to a center ridgeboard or assemble gable-style trusses on the ground and lift them into position. Some lumberyards carry prefabricated trusses for several basic roof spans and pitches.

Measuring Gable Rafters

Because all common rafters in a gable roof are the same, you can mark and cut one, test the fit, and use it as a template.

Three Basic Cuts. Most common rafters get three cuts: a plumb cut at the ridge where the rafter rests against the ridgeboard; a plumb cut

SMART TIP

If you plan on having more than one shed or outbuilding in your yard, make sure they all have the same roof style to achieve a harmonious overall appearance. It is also a good idea to apply the same color and type of roofing material.

at the tail, which makes the shape of the bottom end; and a bird's-mouth cut where the rafter seats on the plate of the outside wall. Sometimes you need a fourth cut, a horizontal cut at the tail, which is often used with an overhang and soffit.

The simplest way to mark these cuts is to hold the lumber up to the ridgeboard, which you can temporarily install on vertical supports. Once the rafter is aligned with the top of

the ridgeboard at one end and resting against the top plate at the other, you can scribe the ridge cut and the seat cut directly onto the rafter. You can also measure these cut lines using a framing square. If you've stepped off the rafter, the first mark you make will be your plumb or ridge cut, the cut that rests against the ridgeboard.

Number of Rafters. If it's not included on your plans, you'll need to calculate the total number of rafters you'll need. For 16-inch-on-center framing, multiply the length of the building by three-quarters, and add 1 (L x 0.75 + 1 = X rafters). For 24-inch-on-center framing, multiply the building length by one-half and add 1 (L x 0.5 + 1 = Y rafters). If your plans include a gable-end overhang to match the eaves overhang, you'll need to add four pieces of lumber for the barge, or fly, rafters that extend beyond the gable-end walls.

Three Methods of Calculating Rafter Length

There are three ways to calculate rafter length, aside from the trusted do-it-yourself method of holding a board in place and marking the cuts. The calculations used here are an example and are not meant for all rafters, but you can use the principles for any common gable rafter.

#1: Using the Pythagorean Theorem

Determine the roof slope. Here, assume a slope of 8 in 12, which means the roof rises 8 inches for every 12 inches it runs. Then determine the building's width. For this example, assume the building is 30 feet wide. Next, determine the run. The run is one-half the building's width, in this case, 15 feet. Finally, determine the rise. Once you know the slope and run, you know the roof will rise 10 feet (8 x 15 = 120 inches, or 10 feet). You're now ready to figure the rafter length for an 8-in-12 roof on a building 30 feet wide. If you think of half the roof as a right triangle, you already know the base (15) and altitude (10). You need to figure the hypotenuse of this right triangle, which represents the rafter length. Using the Pythagorean theorem:

Right Triangle

$$A^2 + B^2 = C^2$$
$$10^2 + 15^2 = C^2$$
$$100 + 225 = 325$$
$$\sqrt{325} = 18.03$$

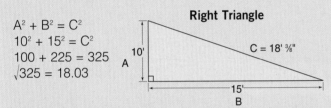

The square root of 325 feet is 18.03 feet, which equals 18 feet ⅜ inch. If your rise and/or run are not in whole feet but in feet and inches, then convert the whole figure to inches; do the math; and convert it back to feet. Use decimals of a foot rather than inches when you divide the resulting number of inches by 12 on a calculator to arrive at feet.

#2: Using a Rafter Table

The rafter table found on a framing square contains work-saving data and is useful for many calculations. You need only look at the first line of the table, which gives unit rafter length for common gable rafters. To find the unit length you need, look on the blade below the inch designation that corresponds to your slope. If, for example, you're framing a 6-in-12 roof, look at the number below the 6-inch mark on the framing square's blade. You'll find it reads 13.42. If your total run is 14, multiply 13.42 by 14 to get 187.88 inches. Divide 187.88 by 12 to get 15.656 feet, or 15 feet 7⅝ inches.

#3: Stepping Off with a Framing Square

You can also accurately measure a rafter by stepping off dimensions using a framing square in 12-inch units of run.

Lay a straight piece of rafter stock across two sawhorses. Sight down the edge of the rafter, and position yourself on the crowned side, which will be the top of the rafter. To make accurate marking easier, attach adjustable stops called stair nuts or stair buttons to the square to set the rise and run positions.

Let's say you want to lay out a roof with an 8-in-12 slope. Lay the square on the left end of the stock. Hold the square's tongue in your left hand and its blade in your right. Pivot the square until the edge of the stock near you aligns with the unit rise mark (8 inches in this example) on the outside of the tongue and the 12-inch mark on the outside of the blade. Mark along the outside edge of the tongue for the ridge plumb line. You'll use this mark as the reference line for stepping off full 12-inch units.

If the span is an odd number of feet, say 25, with a run of 12½ feet, you'll have to include a half-step to accommodate the extra length. Mark off the partial step first, and then go on to step off full 12-inch units. Holding the square in the position in which you had it to mark the ridge cut, measure and mark the length of the odd unit along the blade.

Shift the square to your right along the edge of the stock until the tongue is even with the mark you just made. Mark off a plumb line along the tongue of the square. When you begin stepping off full units, remember to start from the new plumb line and not from the ridge cut line.

Rafter Table

Framing Square

2|3	2|2	2|1	2|0	4 3 2 1

Length Common Rafters Per Foot Run
Length Hip or Valley Per Foot Run
Difference in Length of Jacks 16 Inches Centers
Difference in Length of Jacks 2 Feet Centers
Side Cuts of Jacks Use
Side Cuts of Hip or Valley Use

Rafter Data

Rafter Layout

Partial Step

6"

Framing Square

Rafter

8"

12"

Estimating the Size. Before you order rafter lumber, you must know what size boards to get. You can approximate the sizes using a framing square and measuring tape. To find the exact rafter lengths, you can use any of three methods: work with rafter tables; use the Pythagorean theorem; or step off the rafters with a square. (See "Three Methods of Calculating Rafer Length," opposite.)

To mark rafters, you have to find the roof slope indicated on the building plans. The rafter length will be determined by the roof slope and the building width. The rafter-length measurement will determine where you'll make the cuts on the rafters. The rafter length is the distance from the ridge to the edge of the building. Remember that the rafter size (and wood species and grade) will have to be approved by your local building department.

Subtracting the Ridgeboard Thickness. You start by calculating

the length of the rafter to the center of the ridgeboard. Then you must shorten the rafter to accommodate the width of the board. Measure back from the center of the ridge line a distance of one-half the thickness of the ridgeboard. If you're using a two-by ridgeboard, the distance will be ¾ inch. Mark another plumb line at this point as the cut line.

Calculating the Overhang. The overhang (sometimes called projection) is the level distance from the edge of the building. But the actual rafter length is longer because of its

slope. You can use the Pythagorean theorem to figure out the dimension you'll have to add to the rafter length for the overhang. If you want an 18-inch overhang on the same 8-in-12 roof, for example, you must envision the overhang area as a miniature roof. The run is 18 inches (the horizontal dimension of the overhang) and the rise is 12 inches (8 x 1.5 = 12). Therefore,

$$12^2 + 18^2 = C^2$$
$$144 \text{ inches} + 324 \text{ inches} = 468 \text{ inches}$$

The square root of 468 inches is 21.63 inches, which is 1.80 feet, or 1 foot 9⅝ inches.

The gable end of a roof may also need an overhang to match the eaves overhang. You can create a slight overhang without adding extra rafters. You simply add blocking to the side wall, and add a trim board, often called a rake board. To build a deeper overhang, you can add fly rafters.

SMART TIP

The Pythagorean theorem used to figure rafter length is the same theory behind the 3-4-5 method to determine whether corners are square.

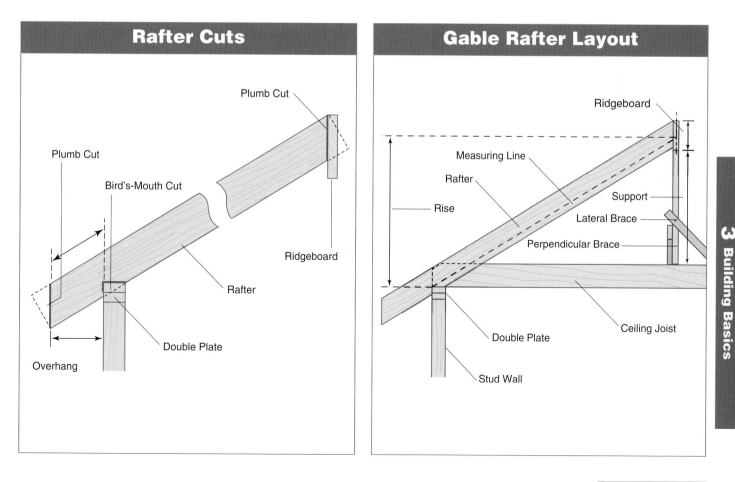

Rafter Cuts

Plumb Cut

Plumb Cut

Bird's-Mouth Cut

Ridgeboard

Rafter

Double Plate

Overhang

Gable Rafter Layout

Ridgeboard

Measuring Line

Rafter

Rise

Support

Lateral Brace

Perpendicular Brace

Double Plate

Ceiling Joist

Stud Wall

Adding Electrical Power

Providing your shed with electrical power will give you the opportunity to install lights and electrical receptacles. The way you plan on using the shed will determine the power requirements, but for most garden sheds, plan on adding a dedicated circuit to the house's existing panel box.

To run electrical power from the main house to your shed, use underground feeder and branch-circuit cable, known as UF cable. It is designated for outdoor wiring because it is weatherproof and suitable for direct burial. The wires are molded into plastic rather than wrapped in paper and then sheathed in plastic as NM cable wires are. Aboveground UF cable must be protected with conduit where subject to damage.

Direct-burial cable must be buried deeply enough to be protected from routine digging. The National Electrical Code specifies minimum depth requirements for underground cable: 24 inches for direct-burial cable; 18 inches for rigid nonmetallic conduit; and 6 inches for rigid and intermediate metal conduit.

If your cable is protected by a GFCI, you may be permitted to trench less deeply, but this is not recommended—you might someday plant a tree or shrub over the cable and risk cutting it while digging.

Any special characteristics of newer types of cable insulation will be identified on the sheathing, such as sunlight and corrosion resistance.

Outdoor Electrical Boxes

There are two main types of outdoor boxes, raintight and watertight. Raintight boxes typically have spring-loaded, self-closing covers, but they are not waterproof. This type of box has a gasket seal and is rated for wet locations as long as the cover is kept closed. It is best to mount a raintight box where it is not subject to water accumulation or flooding. Watertight boxes, on the other hand, are sealed with a waterproof gasket and can withstand a soaking rain or saturation. These boxes are rated for wet locations.

Conduit, Connectors & Fittings

Outdoor wiring is typically protected by rigid conduit—both aboveground and wherever it enters or emerges from underground trenching. Rigid and intermediate metallic conduit (IMC) are most commonly used, but many local codes permit the use of rigid nonmetallic conduit, which is made of polyvinyl chloride (PVC). Regardless of which type of rigid conduit you are permitted to use, you will have to make a variety of connections. These are available for metal and nonmetallic conduit, including bushings for straight pieces and elbow connections, locknuts, offsets, and various couplings. Be sure that the connectors you select match the material and category of conduit you are using.

At the point where cable runs through the exterior wall of your home, you will need a special L-shaped connector called an LB conduit body. An LB encloses the joint between your indoor cable and the outdoor UF cable (UF cable is also permitted for indoor use) that runs down the side of your house and into an underground trench. LB conduit bodies are fitted with a gasket that seals the cable connection against the weather.

Another type of fitting that you may find useful is a box extension which is used to increase the volume of an existing outdoor receptacle or junction box when you need to tap into it to bring power where it is required. This is often done to avoid extensive rewiring and renovation work.

Buried Cable

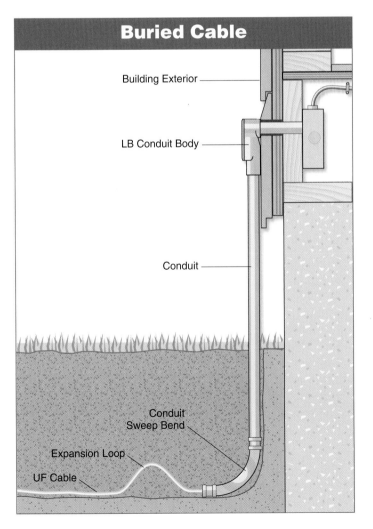

Building Exterior

LB Conduit Body

Conduit

Conduit Sweep Bend

Expansion Loop

UF Cable

Running Cable from the House

1 Mount the junction box over the access opening with screws, and run the branch-circuit cable from the breaker box through the hole on the side of the box.

2 On the outside, use a short length of conduit, called a conduit nipple, to make a connection between the LB fitting and junction box. Turn the long end of the LB fitting down toward the ground.

3 A conduit sweep bend is attached below the first length of conduit. It safeguards the cable as it goes underground. A bushing at the end prevents the cable from chafing.

4 Feed exterior UF cable from the shed up the sweep bend, through the conduit and LB fitting, to the junction box inside. If you need to run conduit through the entire trench, you can do it now.

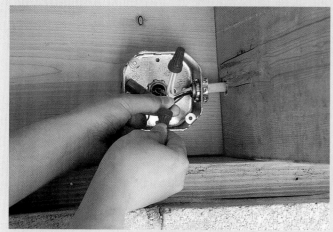

5 Splice the NM cable and exterior UF cable inside the interior junction box, or you can continue the run of cable because UF cable can be used indoors as well.

SMART TIP

At the very least, the shed should have an interior light and an electrical receptacle. It is also convenient to install a GFCI-protected receptacle on the exterior of the building. Of course, if you plan on using the shed as a workshop, you will need more receptacles and a high-amp circuit to accommodate your power tools and other equipment. It is also a good idea to install exterior lights on your shed. Use one to illuminate the entry to the shed and another as security lighting for the yard. For convenience, choose lights that come equipped with motion sensors. The lights will switch on as you approach the shed.

3 Building Basics

saltbox garden shed

Saltbox Garden Shed Diagram

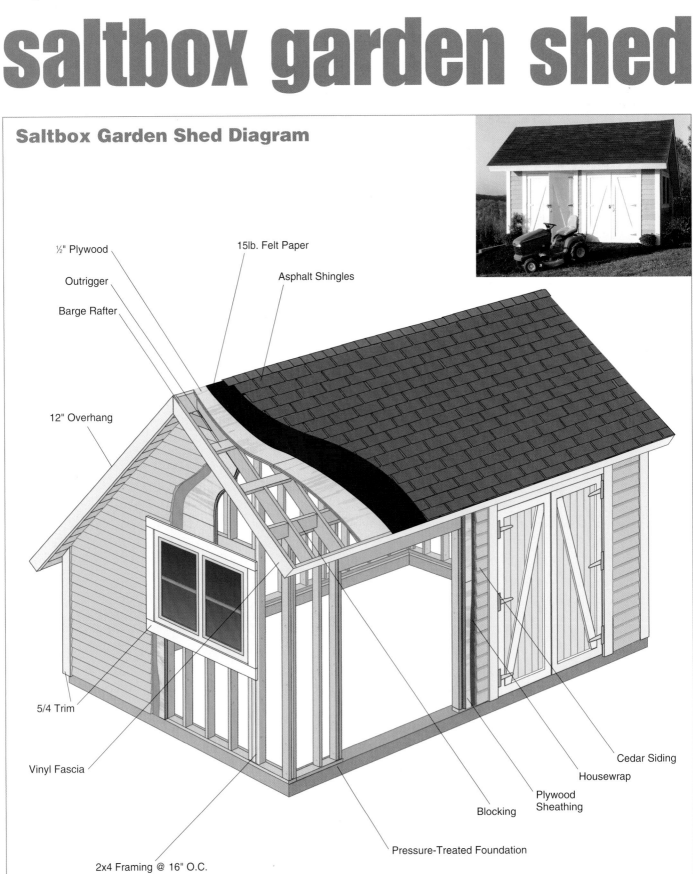

½" Plywood

Outrigger

Barge Rafter

12" Overhang

15lb. Felt Paper

Asphalt Shingles

5/4 Trim

Vinyl Fascia

2x4 Framing @ 16" O.C.

Blocking

Pressure-Treated Foundation

Plywood Sheathing

Housewrap

Cedar Siding

Building the Shed

If you are going to build a shed from scratch, it should not look like a prefabricated shed that you bought and had delivered, all assembled, to your site. This one differs markedly from a prefab in appearance, spaciousness, and construction. And it will last as long as your house does.

Inside the shed, you have a generous overhead space and ample floor space for a garden bench and storage shelves. And of course, it's the perfect shed for parking your lawn tractor and trailer, wheelbarrow, shredder, snowblower, string trimmer, leaf blower, and full complement of shovels, rakes, and pruners. The windows and doors let in plenty of light, so you won't lose small tools in dark corners.

Design Basics. The shed measures 12 x 16 feet, with two pairs of wide, hinged doors and windows in both end walls. The walls are framed with 2x4s, with ½-inch plywood or OSB sheathing. The siding is beveled western red cedar; the painted wood trim is ¾ pine.

The shed is built on a foundation of 6x6 pressure-treated timbers set on a gravel footing. The floor is compacted screenings, or fine gravel. The screenings can be wet down and compacted to form a smooth, hard surface. This circumvents the labor and expense of building a concrete slab.

Roofing. The height of the roof ridge presents the biggest challenge, and using scaffolding is essential. After you have framed and erected the front and back walls, set up your scaffolding in the center of the floor to install the rafters.

Materials List

Foundation
8 pcs.	6x6	16'
8 pcs.	6x6	12'
84 spikes	10" galvanized	
20 rebar spikes	18"	
gravel		
screenings		

Framing and Sheathing
28 sheets ½" CDX plywood
2 pcs.	2x10	10'
19 pcs.	2x8	12'
19 pcs.	2x8	8'
3 pcs.	2x6	12'
7 pcs.	2x4	16'
5 pcs.	2x4	14'
12 pcs.	2x4	12'
28 pcs.	2x4	10'
11 pcs.	2x4	8'
4 pcs.	1x8	10' No. 2 pine

12d common nails
8d common nails

Roofing
9 pcs. aluminum drip edge, 10' long
3 rolls, 15 lb. builder's felt
  (total of 296 needed for roof and walls)
13 bundles of shingles
  (3 bundles per square)
⅞" roofing nails
⅝" staples
2 tubes asphalt cement

Windows
4 double-hung windows, 34" x 36"

Trim Boards
15 pcs.	⅝ x6	12' No. 2 pine
6 pcs.	⅝ x6	14' No. 2 pine
6 pcs.	1x6	12' No. 2 pine
6 pcs.	1x8	10' No. 2 pine

12d finish nails
3 tubes latex caulk
1 gal. latex exterior primer
1 gal. latex exterior paint

Soffits and Fascia
13 pcs. vinyl soffit, 12' long
8 pcs. vinyl fascia, 12' long
8 pcs. vinyl J-channel
aluminum trim nails

Siding
1060 lin. ft. ½" x 8" western red cedar beveled siding
2" aluminum siding nails
1¼" stainless-steel screws
1 gal. latex semitransparent exterior stain

Doors
4 shts.	¾" exterior birch plywood	
13 pcs.	1x6	8' No. 2 pine
1 pc.	1x8	8' No. 2 pine

2 tubes construction adhesive
6d finishing nails
12 T-hinges
48 screws, 3" No. 12
48 hex bolts w/washers, split washers, and nuts, ⁵⁄₁₆" x 2"
2 clasps and staples w/mounting screws
2 sliding bolts w/mounting screws

Building the Foundation

The saltbox shed is built on a perimeter foundation composed of 6x6 pressure-treated timbers spiked together with 10-inch galvanized nails. It's a practical, easy-to-construct foundation that even a lone builder can complete, though it sure is nice to have some help hefting the timbers.

It's important to extend the foundation down below the frost line and to promote drainage away from the foundation. You can hire an excavator to dig the foundation trenches and strip the sod from the interior area using a backhoe. The work takes well under half a day.

Spread gravel in the trenches; then lay the first course of timbers. Naturally, the number of courses needed depends on how deep your trenches are. The goal is to have the top surface of the foundation just a few inches above grade.

Take the time to do a good job of leveling and squaring the first course. Having to compensate for a pitched, out-of-square base will make it difficult to frame a square and plumb shed.

1 Use two tape measures and the 3-4-5 methods to lay out the foundation corners. When the 16-ft. side and the 12-ft. side are laid out at right angles, the diagonal measure will be 20 ft.

4 Drive rebar pins through the first-course timbers to tie them to the ground. Drill a pilot hole completely through the timber; then hammer the 24-in.-long pin in place using a hand sledge.

5 Build up the foundation with the timbers alternating at the corners. Position all four timbers for a course, and measure the diagonals to ensure the course is square. Drill a pilot hole; then spike the new course to the one below using 10-in. galvanized nails.

2 Mark the outside corners of the foundation trenches on the ground using fluorescent spray paint. Nothing more is needed for an excavation job this simple.

3 Shovel gravel into the trenches to promote drainage. You need a layer about 6 in. deep all around. Level the gravel's surface as much as possible before setting the first-course timbers in place.

6 Backfill the trenches as soon as you can. Shovel a layer of soil into the gap between the trench wall and the foundation; then tamp it. Backfill more, and tamp again. Because the soil will settle, backfill a few inches above grade.

7 Have the screenings or fine gravel dumped directly into the foundation, if possible. As you spread and level the material, tamp it methodically, either by hand, as shown, or with a power tamper.

Framing the Back Wall

Because of the saltbox roofline, the roof is framed after the front and back walls are up but before the side walls are framed. The side-wall studs extend from the sill to the rafters, and they are cut and fastened one at a time.

In general, you frame a wall by cutting the parts, laying them out on a flat surface, and nailing them together. You nail the sheathing to the frame while it's still lying flat, primarily because it's easier to do this way. Also, it enables you to square the wall assembly before erecting it. The sheathing will keep the wall assembly square as you heave it into place.

Choose long, straight 2x4s for the plates. Set the top plates and soleplates side by side. Mark up the plates together, but on each, mark only the locations of studs that actually abut it. Code the location according to the type of stud that goes there. For example, use an "S" for a full-length stud, a "C" for a cripple, and a "T" for a trimmer.

That done, cut studs and trimmers to length, and make up your corner posts and any headers needed.

Framing. Lay the frame parts for a wall on the shed floor. Line up the studs, and arrange one plate across the bottoms, the other across the tops. Drive 16d nails through the plates into the ends of each stud.

Measure the frame, and cut pieces of ½-inch CDX plywood to size. Don't worry about openings for windows or doors; you'll cut them out after nailing the sheathing to the studs. Extend the plywood 1 inch beyond the bottom plate so that it will overlap the seam between the plate and the foundation. Leave a ⅛-inch gap between pieces, and of course, size the pieces so joints between them will occur over a stud.

Next, you must set up the wall and brace it. This job requires at least two people. First of all, the wall is heavy, and once it is upright, you will need at least one person to hold it up while the other gets the bottom aligned properly on the foundation and sets up the bracing.

Once the wall is braced, drive 16d nails through the soleplate into the foundation.

1 Lay out the top and soleplates for the back wall together. Measure and mark the stud locations, and mark an "X" on the side of the line where the stud will be attached.

4 Take the diagonal measurements to ensure the frame is square. You can shift the alignment of the assembly by rapping a corner with a sledge hammer. Swing the hammer as you would a putter in golf.

2 Pile identical studs with their ends flush. Mark a cut line on the top layer of studs. As you cut through the top studs, you'll kerf those underneath, marking where they are to be cut.

3 Line up the plates and studs, and drive nails through the plate into the end of each stud. Use foot pressure to align the top surfaces as you drive the nails.

5 Nail the plywood sheathing to the frame once it is square. The job is easier with the frame lying flat. The sheathing prevents the wall from shifting out of square as you lift it into position.

6 Set up the frame, and brace it. The job requires at least two: one to hold the wall and monitor the level, the other to nail the brace to the foundation.

1 Mark up the top and soleplates together, but on each, mark only the locations of studs that actually abut it. Code the location according to the type of stud that goes there.

2 Build up a header by face-nailing two 2x8s together, with a ½-in. plywood spacer between them. The plywood doesn't have to be a continuous piece; this is a good place to use up scraps.

5 Sheathe the wall frame after squaring it. Apply full sheets of plywood, covering up the top portion of the doorways. After the wall is sheathed, snap cut lines and cut out the doorways.

6 Raise the wall into position. It is heavy; you'll need a strong helper or two to tip it up. Once the wall is tipped up, it takes little effort to hold it upright.

3 Face-nail the trimmers to full-length studs, and make up corner posts by face-nailing studs together. You can economize by sandwiching short pieces of 2x4 between the studs to form the corner posts.

4 Lay the wall frame parts on the shed floor for assembly. One by one, line up the parts on the appropriate layout lines, and nail through the plates into the ends of the studs.

7 Install temporary bracing to hold the wall erect. Nail 2x4s to the corner posts and to scraps scabbed to the foundation, as shown. Make sure the wall is plumb.

Front Wall Frame

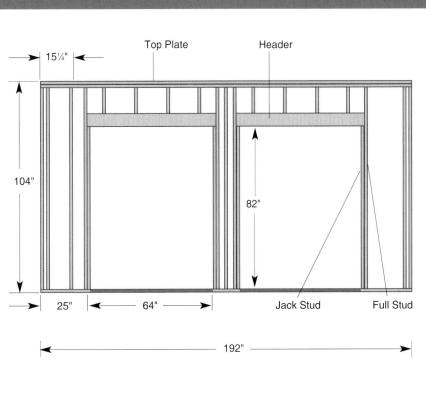

Top Plate   Header

15¼"

104"

82"

25"   64"

Jack Stud   Full Stud

192"

Roof Framing

The biggest challenge in building the saltbox shed is framing the roof, and there are a couple of reasons for this. Because the ridge beam is longer than any standard board, you'll have to join two pieces end to end, and you will have to make the connection about 12 feet above the sill. Finally, because the shed is saltbox style, the front rafters are different from the back rafters.

You have to deal with the ridge first. Get it up, and then you can cut and fit a front rafter and a back rafter. Use the first two rafters as patterns to lay out the remaining rafters.

Unless you have several helpers, it's easiest to splice the ridgeboard after you hoist the two sections into place atop temporary supports. But lay out the rafter locations while the ridgeboard sections are on the ground (or on sawhorses, anyway). Select straight boards and prepare two splice boards, which you'll scab across the end-to-end butt joint, once the sections are aloft. The splice should fall between rafters.

Setting up temporary supports for the ridgeboard requires some ingenuity. Because the end walls aren't framed yet, you have to stand a long stud on the foundation and attach braces at right angles to hold it erect. A similar stud must be erected and braced midway between the end supports. You don't want the supports to interfere with the rafters or the splice.

Stretch a level line across the braces, and scab a 2x4 scrap to each stud. You rest the ridge on these supports and clamp it to the stud, which should extend up past the ridge. (See page 58.) After the ridge sections are clamped to the studs, attach the splice boards.

While there are a couple of methods for laying out rafters, the best for this project is the step-off, which uses a framing square. The procedure is depicted in the drawings below. (For general guidelines for cutting and installing rafters, see "Three Methods for Calculating Rafter Length," page 44.)

Two front and two back rafters must be notched for outriggers to which the barge rafters are attached. The barge rafters form the roof overhang. The barge rafters—two front ones and two back ones—are characterized by the absence of the bird's mouth. As you install the rafters, you place the notched ones flush with the ends of the walls. The outriggers set into the notches, and you nail through the adjacent rafters into their ends. The barge rafters are nailed to the ridge and to the outriggers.

Complete the roof framing by nailing blocking between the rafters, flush with the outside of the front and back walls. You can face-nail through the rafter for one side of the blocking and toenail the other side of the blocking. Cut and install the collar ties. Finally, cut and nail fascia boards spanning the overhanging ends of the rafters at the front and back. The fascia is a nice design detail, and its installation helps to hold the rafters in place, adding support to the entire roof assembly.

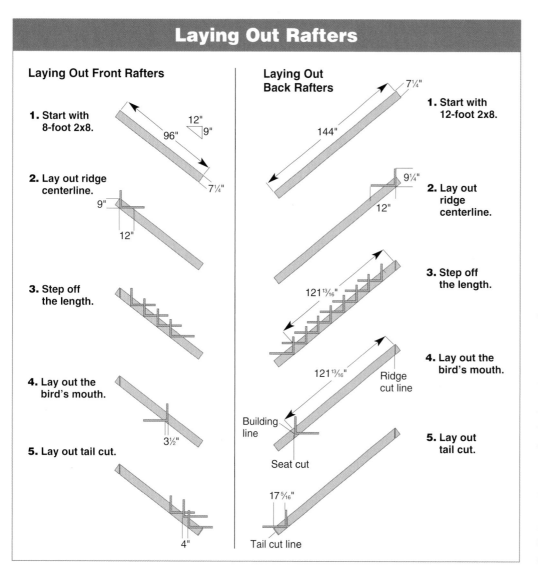

Laying Out Rafters

Laying Out Front Rafters

1. Start with 8-foot 2x8.
96"   12" / 9"   7¼"

2. Lay out ridge centerline.
9"   12"

3. Step off the length.

4. Lay out the bird's mouth.
3½"

5. Lay out tail cut.
4"

Laying Out Back Rafters

1. Start with 12-foot 2x8.
144"   7¼"

2. Lay out ridge centerline.
9¼"   12"

3. Step off the length.
121¹³⁄₁₆"

4. Lay out the bird's mouth.
121¹³⁄₁₆"   Ridge cut line
Building line
Seat cut

5. Lay out tail cut.
17⁵⁄₁₆"
Tail cut line

Framing the Roof

1 Mark the ridge centerline, then offset to locate the ridge cut line. Then use your framing square to step off the length of the rafter and to locate the building line.

2 Lay out the seat cut by aligning the framing square's tongue on the building line and the 4-in. mark on the blade with the rafter edge. Scribe along the blade.

3 Use the first rafter cut that fits just right as a pattern for laying out the others. Align the rafter on a 2x8, and trace the ridge cut and the bird's mouth.

4 Mark off the rafter locations on the ridge. Measure from the scarf-joint bevel on each of the two 2x8 ridge sections. Mark both sides of the ridge. *(continued on page 58)*

(continued from page 57)

Framing the Roof

5 Erect temporary supports for the ridge. Use chalk-line string to align the "seats" for the ridge atop the supports. Clamp the two ridge sections onto the supports.

6 The first rafter to abut the ridge at each location can be face-nailed in place. Drive three nails through the ridge into the end of the rafter.

9 Close in the spaces between rafters with blocking. Rip a bevel on a 2x8; then crosscut it into blocking. Face-nail through one rafter into the blocking, and toenail through the other.

10 With the collar tie resting on the front top plate, level it; then face-nail a collar tie to the back rafter. Then go back to the front end and face-nail the tie to the rafter and toenail it to the top plate.

7 The second rafter at each location must be toenailed to the ridge. Drive a nail through the top edge of the rafter into the ridge, and toenail through each side as well.

8 Toenail each rafter to the top plate using 16d nails. Drive nails into both faces of the rafter, angling each down into the plate.

11 For the outriggers, clamp both rafters face to face, and cut the outrigger notches in both at the same time. Remove the bulk of the waste using your circular saw. Then chisel the bottom of the notches flat.

12 Fit the outriggers into the notches, and pull their ends tight to the adjacent rafter. Drive two 16d nails through the outrigger into the rafter. Face-nail through the rafter into the end of the outrigger.

Framing the End Walls

1 Setting temporary braces against the front and back walls during construction of the end walls is prudent. Nail a scrap to the wall; then butt a brace underneath it. Nail the brace to a stake in the ground.

2 One by one, stand the end-wall studs on the soleplate markings, and mark along the underside of the rafter on its edge. Use a level to ensure that the stud is plumb as you mark it.

5 Plumb the stud; then drive a couple of 12d nails through the stud into the rafter.

6 Cripples are studs that extend from the soleplate to the rough sill. After the sill is set, stand the cripples one by one on the layout marks on the plate and face-nail through the sill into their ends. With the tops thus secured, it is easier to toenail the bottom ends to the plate.

3 Cut the notch using your circular saw. After making the angled shoulder cut across the stud's edge, rip in from the end to that cut.

4 Toenailing a stud to the soleplate is easy if the stud is braced against a block. Then the hammer blows won't move it off its mark.

7 The header, made up of two 2x8s and some plywood scraps, rests on trimmers that extend up from the rough sill. Set the header in place, and face-nail through the full-length stud into it. Use 16d nails.

8 More cripples extend from the header to the rafters. Mark and notch these, and stand them in place. Face-nail them to the rafter; toenail them to the header.

Sheathing the End Walls

1 Temporarily nail a ledger to the foundation to support the ½-in. plywood sheets at the correct height. Set a sheet on the ledger; align it left and right; then nail it to the studs.

2 With the first three sheets in place, take measurements from the shed, and use them to lay out the piece of sheathing that fits the triangular gable end. The piece fits against the underside of the outriggers. The notch accommodates the ridge.

3 From inside the shed, drill a hole through the sheathing at each corner of the rough openings for the windows. Draw or snap lines from hole to hole; then saw on the lines to remove the sheathing.

Sheathing the Roof

1 The barge rafter is beyond the side wall, hanging on the ends of the outriggers. Use ¾ pine for this because it presents a far better appearance than many of the 2x8s that are available.

2 Nail the fascia board to the ends of the rafters. Join the fascia boards in a scarf joint, and locate the joint on the end of rafter.

3 Begin sheathing the roof at the lowest end. After the first sheets are nailed down, nail a 2x4 to the rafters to provide footing. Add 2x4s as you add the second row of plywood sheets, and so on up the roof. The sheets should be nailed to the rafters using 8d common nails.

Shingling the Roof

A straightforward roofing job like this one requires only a tape measure, chalk line, hammer, roofer's knife, stapler for the roofing felt, and metal shears to cut the drip edge. While a pneumatic roofing nailer does speed up the work, and you can rent both the compressor and the nail gun, the saltbox shed isn't really a large job. The labor saved may not offset the cost of the rental and the time spent picking up and dropping off the equipment.

From both safety and efficiency standpoints, scaffolding is essential because you want to be able to work along the eaves from rake to rake. Roofing jacks are a worthwhile investment. Four can be spaced across the roof to support a work platform to be used when the shingle course is out of reach from the scaffolding.

Roofing the shed is not complicated. You stretch strips of roofing felt from rake to rake and staple them to the sheathing. Begin at the eave and work up the slope.

1 Staple builder's felt to the roof. Cut the strips to span the full width of the roof. Align the first strip with the bottom edge of the roof, and staple it down. The second course should overlap the first by 4 to 6 in.

4 Lay the first full course of shingles with the tabs overlaying the starter course. Follow the nailing pattern specified by the manufacturer on the packaging. Typically, you use four nails per shingle, positioning them above the notch between tabs.

5 Begin the next several courses. The notches between tabs must be staggered from course to course, so you must cut down the first shingle in six of every seven courses. The second course begins with a 2½-tab shingle, the third with a 2-tab shingle.

2 Install drip edge to protect the edges of the sheathing. Along the lower edge of the roof, the roofing felt overlaps the drip edge. Along the gable edges, install the drip edge overlapping the felt.

3 Begin shingling the roof with a starter course. Cut the tabs off shingles. Invert the tab-free strips and position them along the roof edge.

6 As you progress up the roof, use roofing jacks to create a work platform. For each jack, drive a framing nail through the body of a shingle and into a rafter. Leave the head protruding so that you can catch the jack on the nail. Two jacks are sufficient to support an 8-ft. 2x6.

7 Remove the jacks when the roofing is complete by rolling back the tab and unhooking the jack. Seat the nail and cover the head with a dab of roofing asphalt. Roll the tab back down.

Installing the Windows

1 Wrap the shed in builder's felt, extending the strips around the corners and across the rough openings for the windows. Each strip overlaps the one below it. Strips lap end to end, too. Staple the felt to the plywood. At the rough openings, slice through the felt using a utility knife.

2 Fold flaps of the felt over the edges of the rough window openings, and staple them to the studs, sill, and header.

3 Install the windows in the rough openings. Stand a unit on the sill and align it laterally. Then tip it up and into the opening. Make sure the nailing flange seats against the shed walls all around. Have a helper inside the shed plumb the unit with shims.

4 Drive nails through the nailing flange into the framing of the rough opening. Most windows have punched holes in the flange to indicate where to locate the nails.

Trimming the Soffits and Fascia

1 Close in the eaves with vinyl soffit panels. Under the front and rear overhangs, the panels run across the rafters. Nail them to the bottom edges of the rafters. At the gable ends, fasten nailers to the sidewalls parallel with the barge rafters.

2 Cut and mount short pieces of soffit to the gable end eaves. Cut the vinyl using a jigsaw or circular saw. Hook the bottom of the soffit into the interlock bead on the previously installed piece. Slide the piece along the bead to the wall.

3 Attach the soffit. Pull the piece tight, ensuring it is hooked to its neighbor; then drive aluminum or galvanized roofing nails through the nailing slots. A nail into the nailer and one into the rafter will hold it.

4 Cover the barge rafters and fascia boards with vinyl fascia. The lip on the fascia strip overlaps the soffit ends, and the top edge fits under the roof drip edge.

Trimming the Windows, Doors, and Corners

The trim applied to the saltbox shed is a significant part of its traditional design. The windows and doors are framed with wide boards, and matching boards are applied at the corners. To produce the desired appearance, use ⁵⁄₄ stock for this trim. Typically ⁵⁄₄ pine is 1 to 1³⁄₁₆ inches thick, and usually is stocked in standard nominal widths from 4 to 12 inches.

The trim is applied after the shed has been wrapped with felt paper or housewrap and the soffits have been trimmed out. Cut and fit the boards tight around the windows and the doorjambs. You will probably get the best fit around the windows if you cut rabbets in the trim to accommodate the nailing flange of the window. As you cut each part, tack it in place to test fit.

Before nailing the trim firmly in place, pull it down and prime the boards—front, back, ends, and edges. When the primer is dry, nail up the trim. Chalk the seam between the trim and the windows. Apply at least one finish coat to all exposed surfaces. The shed is ready for siding.

1 Place the prefitted, preassembled, preprimed corner board. The board that seats against the gable-end soffit is mitered. The adjoining board is beveled at the same angle. Nail the two together, and prime them.

4 Cut and fit the window trim; then prime it. If necessary, mill a rabbet into the back of each trim strip to accommodate the nailing flange so the board lies flat against the sheathing. A rabbet in the face may be needed to fit the board into the window's siding channel.

5 Set the header trim atop the windows. Align it laterally, and seat it tight against the windows. Fit the vertical trim on either side of the windows. Again, be sure it is seated tight against the window and against the header.

2 With the corner-board assembly square against the shed walls and tight against the soffits, fasten it using 12d finishing nails. Be sure the nails penetrate the corner posts of the shed.

3 Before casing in the doorways, you must cut the sole-plate out. Use a handsaw to cut flush with the studs on either side of the doorway.

6 Nail the trim to the shed using 12d finishing nails. Use a nail set to countersink the heads. Finish the installation by filling the nailholes with putty, sanding, and priming the repairs before applying a finish coat of paint.

SMART TIP

Prime trim before nailing it in place. It is best to apply a coat of primer on both front and back and the edges, including the end grain. The primer acts as a sealer that helps prevent the wood from absorbing moisture.

Siding the Shed

A lot of different siding materials are available. Beveled-wood siding is especially attractive and reasonably durable. However, the siding itself is more expensive than most other sidings, and it can be time-consuming to install. If you are building the shed yourself and you enjoy the work, time shouldn't be a major consideration, though, should it?

Western red cedar siding is used on the saltbox shed. Western red cedar is one of those woods that weathers extremely well. The siding is ½ inch (at the thicker edge) x 8 inches wide. Typically, it's delivered in random lengths, ranging in 1-foot increments from 4 feet up to 16 feet. An alternative to this siding is cedar shingles.

Cedar splits easily, so exercise care in handling and cutting it. Drill a pilot hole for every fastener you drive.

You can paint or stain cedar, and it's a good idea to apply stain or primer to the front and back before installing the siding. If you leave it natural, it will darken markedly as it weathers.

1 Begin siding the shed by nailing a starter strip at the bottom of a wall. The width of the strip equals the siding overlap. Use the thin top edge of damaged siding pieces for the starter strip. Align the starter strip flush with the bottom ends of the corner boards.

4 Notching a single siding strip to fit beneath and above windows and doors is more work. Layout must be accurate, and the strip can be difficult to maneuver into position without breaking. But the payoff is a better-looking job. The alternative is to use two strips to make up the course.

2 Install the first strip of full-width siding over the starter strip. Cut it to fit tight between the corner boards. While you might opt to use two pieces to form a single course here and there as you advance up the wall, it's best to use a single strip for the first course.

3 Cedar splinters easily. Scoring the cut line with a utility knife pays dividends—especially when the siding is pre-finished—in practically eliminating the splintering. A power miter saw makes fast crosscuts, but a jigsaw is useful for notching strips as well as crosscutting them.

5 Drill a pilot hole for every nail you drive through the siding. Cedar splits easily. A simple gauge aligns the bit in relation to the edge, so all the nailheads are in a line. Snap chalk lines on the builder's felt to mark stud locations.

Nailing Siding

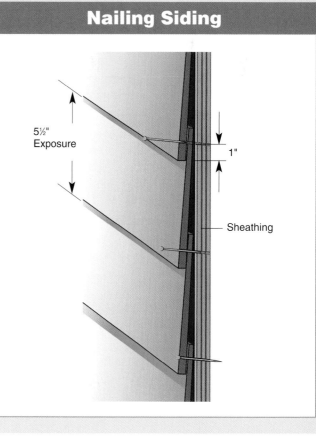

5½" Exposure

1"

Sheathing

Building and Hanging the Doors

1 Build each door by attaching a wooden frame to a plywood panel. After cutting the plywood to size, use a router and V-grooving bit to cut grooves in the panel's face. Clamp a straightedge to the plywood, and guide the router along it.

2 Lay out and trim the diagonal brace for the frame before assembly. Rip and crosscut the vertical and horizontal frame members to size. Line up these parts on the plywood, and secure them using a pipe clamp at each end. Position the roughly sized diagonal brace, and clamp it.

5 Clamp the parts to one another and to the plywood while the adhesive sets. A pipe clamp applied across the vertical frame members pinches them against the ends of the horizontal parts. Bar clamps and C-clamps squeeze the parts against the face of the plywood. While the parts are clamped, drive and countersink nails.

6 Shellac any knots before priming and painting the doors. Use a dewaxed or pigmented shellac for this job. These sealers, which dry quickly, prevent the knot from bleeding through the paint. Apply a couple of coats just to the knots and pitch pockets; then prime and paint the entire door.

3 Mark the intersection of the brace and the horizontal frame piece. Set a sliding bevel to the angle as shown— the tool's body against the horizontal piece, its blade against the brace. Use this angle to scribe a cut line from the mark across the brace piece.

4 Assemble the frame to the door panel using construction adhesive and nails. The end-to-edge joints between the frame members and the brace can be aligned using biscuits. Dry assemble the parts, and clamp them. One by one, unclamp the parts, and apply construction adhesive to their backs.

7 Fit the doors, with T-hinges mounted, into the door-ways, one by one, so that you can mark the hinge locations on the jambs. A permanent stop nailed to the head jamb and a temporary one tacked to the sill locate the door. Set the bottom of the door on a shim, and slide it against the side jamb.

Door Layout

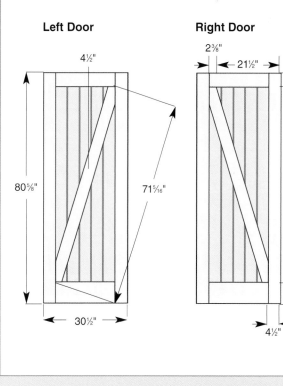

Left Door

4½"

80⅝"

71⁵⁄₁₆"

30½"

Right Door

2⅜"

21½"

5⅜"

7¼"

4½"

gambrel yard shed

Gambrel Yard Shed Diagram

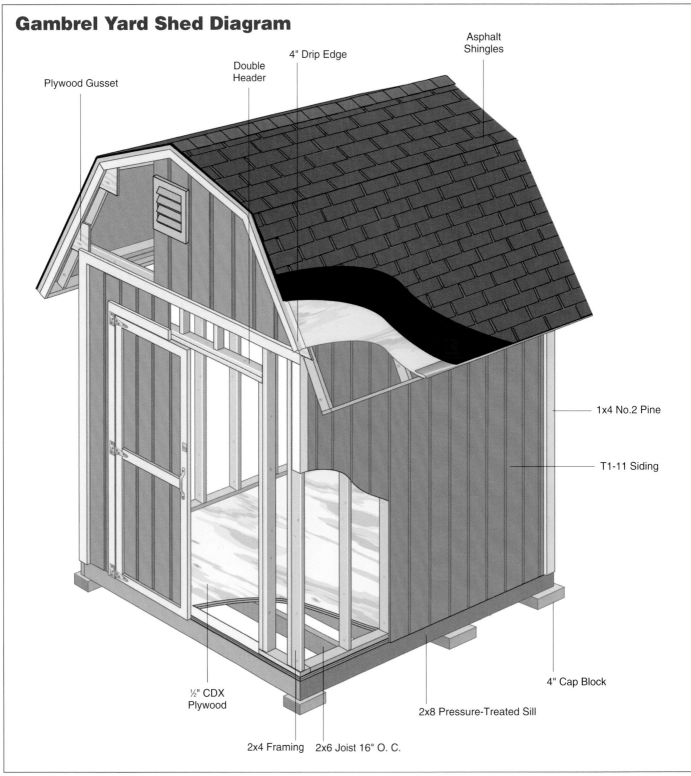

Plywood Gusset

Double Header

4" Drip Edge

Asphalt Shingles

1x4 No.2 Pine

T1-11 Siding

4" Cap Block

2x8 Pressure-Treated Sill

½" CDX Plywood

2x4 Framing

2x6 Joist 16" O. C.

Building the Gambrel Yard Shed

The design shown here is a gambrel shed. It has the same walls and floors as most other buildings, but it is distinguished by its gambrel roof. A gambrel roof is really a combination of two roofs of varying pitches. In this design, the lower portion of the roof has a steep pitch, while the upper part of the roof has a pitch that is not as steep as the lower section.

Though many people prefer the crisp lines of a gable roof, a gambrel roof is ideal for a shed because it provides a great deal of storage space in the "second story" (the space created by the high-pitched rafters) even though the shed is nominally a one-story structure.

The rafters of this gambrel shed were created using site-built trusses. The bottom chords of the trusses—the 2x4s that span from wall to wall and form the bottom of the truss—provide an area on which you can lay plywood to create a platform storage area, or you can use the space to hold spare lumber or items that are otherwise hard to store.

The gambrel shed shown in this

chapter is 8 x 8 feet, with a substantial overhang on either end of the roof to keep water away from the siding and the foundation blocks. Using standard dimensions like these reduces the cutting of dimension lumbers and sheetgoods (plywood roof decking and siding), which come in 8-foot lengths.

Framing. The gambrel shed is framed with 2-by lumber 16 inches on center. The floor joists are made of pressure-treated wood because there is a good chance that they will come in direct contact with water

from rain, runoff, and melting snow. But note that the siding is T1-11 siding, which is typically plywood. It may also be oriented-strand board, also called OSB. OSB is a patchwork of wood held in place by strong adhesive. T1-11 has grooves cut into its finished side (the side that will

face outside) to give it the look of board-and-batten siding. T1-11's structural composition is similar to that of ½-inch CDX plywood, but unlike ordinary plywood sheathing, it can be painted and does not require additional finishing, as does clapboard or shingle siding.

Materials List

Foundation

2	50-lb bags of ¾" gravel
10	4" cap blocks
12 tubes	construction adhesive
2 pcs.	2x8 8' pressure treated
4 pcs.	2x4 8' pressure treated
10 pcs.	2x6 8' pressure treated

Framing and Sheathing

11 sheets	½" CDX plywood
24 pcs.	2x4 8' SPF
10 sheets	4x8 T1-11 Siding
14 pcs.	2x4 10'
2 louver vents	16" x 20"
8d common nails	
12d common nails	

Roofing

6	4" wide drip edge (10' lengths)
1 roll	100' 10# roofing felt
6 bundles	3-tab asphalt shingles
⅞" roofing nails	

Trim Boards

20 pcs. 1x4 8' No. 2 pine trim

Stairs

4	4" cap blocks
2 pcs.	2x8 10' pressure treated
4 pcs.	2x6 8' pressure treated

Doors

8 pcs. 2x4 8' (for frame)

Finishing

6	tubes of latex caulk
1	gal. primer
2	gal. paint

Framing the Floor

Like the other sheds presented in this book, the gambrel shed sits on a foundation of stacked 4-inch solid concrete blocks. The blocks rest on crushed stone that goes down 8 inches. The stone base drains the area around the concrete blocks. Stone is also a useful tool in leveling the blocks as you can use the gravel to shim the blocks as necessary. Be sure to check with the building inspector in your area. Some codes require that sheds have a foundation that extends below the frost line.

Though the first block sits directly on the crushed stone, the remaining blocks should be glued together with standard construction adhesive, which you apply with your caulking gun. It is important that the block layout will provide you with a base to build a shed that is both level and square. Any deviation at this stage will result in your mistakes being highly visible when the building is complete. After setting the blocks, make sure that they form a square.

1 Check that the blocks create a square. Measure from the center of one block to the center of another that is diagonally across from it. If this measurement matches the other diagonal span, the base is square.

4 Once you place the 2x6 floor joists 16 in. on center, use galvanized nails to nail into the ends of the joists. Do not toenail from inside into the rim joist. You may have to shim to bring the joists flush with the rim joists.

5 Apply a bead of construction adhesive to the tops of all the rim and floor joists. This will glue the plywood in place and give the floor a firmer feel. Otherwise, the floor can feel springy.

2 Once the blocks are level, set 2x8 pressure-treated rim joists in place. The 2x4 ledgers hold the joists upright while you get them level and properly positioned.

3 Because this shed is 8 x 8 ft., foundation blocks are used just in the corners, and pressure-treated 2x8 rim joists are used to form the floor frame for the shed.

6 Screw the deck in place, attaching screws every 6 in. around the perimeter and every 12 in. along the interior joists. Note that an 8 x 8-ft. floor takes exactly two sheets of plywood.

7 Snapping chalk lines over the joists will guide you for screw placement. If you do this "by eye," with no line to guide you, you may not get the screws dead center into the joists.

Building the Walls

1 Lay out stud walls on the floor deck, which can serve as a good, solid, level working surface. Mark the location of each stud on the plates ahead of time.

2 There is no need to use galvanized nails for wood framing if the nails will be covered by the roof. Nail through the top plate into the end grain of the wall studs. Use two nails per stud.

4 One person can easily raise an 8-ft. stud wall, but notice that a brace is in place and nailed with one nail into the side of the rim joist. This will serve to hold the wall in place once it is erected.

5 Using a 4-ft. level, check the wall for plumb. Once it is plumb, drive a single nail through the brace into the end 2x4 on the wall. Don't drive the nail all the way home because you will remove the brace once the adjacent wall is in place.

The Walls

The walls of this gambrel shed were framed with SPF (spruce-pine-fir) 2x4 lumber. Gang-cut the 8-foot-long studs to trim 3 inches off of each. That will allow the 8-foot sheets of T1-11 siding to extend beyond the bottom of each wall. When the wall is standing upright, the T1-11 will partially overlap the rim joist and protect it from the elements.

Because the wall is 8 feet long and the framing was done 16 inches on center, the wall is composed of exactly six symmetrical stud bays. Where possible, sheathe the walls when the stud frame is lying down because it is easier to get the edges of the T1-11 to match exactly the edges of the 2x4s. However, it is more difficult to lift a fully sheathed wall into position. This shed is relatively small, so the average person should be able to handle the task. But working with at least one other person will make the job easier.

Unless you plan to finish the inside walls of the shed by applying drywall or paneling, the end studs of each wall can simply abut one another; you do not have to configure a corner to create a nailing surface for interior finishes. If you do want to finish the interior, use one of the corner framing methods described in "Stud Configurations at Corners," page 40.

3 With the wall framed and all nailed up, lay a piece of T1-11 siding in place. Use the edges of the siding to help square up the stud wall.

6 With the opposing wall erected, check all walls for plumb, and then attach adjacent walls to one another. Nail through the bottom plates into the rim joist as well, using one nail per stud bay.

Which Wall First?

For this type of construction, it is best to build walls in opposing pairs. We started with the side walls of the shed. Building walls in this way allows you to construct the wall on the floor of the shed, including adding the wall sheathing, and then lifting the wall into place. At this point, make sure the wall is plumb and square. Constructing the opposite wall second provides an unobstructed path to frame, sheathe, and lift the second wall into position. With two opposing side walls in place, you can add the walls that fit between them, although you may find it easier to frame these walls in place.

Making and Installing Trusses

Trusses are a great way to frame a roof because they can be mass-produced on the ground, reducing your time on a ladder, and they bring a crisp consistency to the roofline that might be hard to attain for the beginning roof framer using stick framing. You can stick-frame the gambrel roof, as you would for a gable roof, but the geometry on a gambrel is complicated. Plus, the configuration of the truss chords, and the support each member of the truss provides, brings a natural stability to a roof truss that is hard to obtain with stick-framed rafters.

Making the Trusses. Though trusses can be ordered through your local lumberyard, they are not hard to make on the job site. Because you construct them using 2x4 lumber—not the 2x6s or 2x8s required for freestanding rafters—they are not expensive to construct.

The best way to make trusses on-site is to cut and lay out one ideal truss and assemble it on the shed floor. Once you know you have the angles right, gang-cut the remaining chords so that you can set up an assembly line to make a number of trusses at once.

For this shed, the bottom cord is 8 feet long; the rise is 4 feet. The lower cord is at a 60-degree angle to the bottom cord; the upper cord is at a 30-degree angle. Before installing trusses, have a number of shorter 2x4s ready to act as braces. Cut a 4- and 6-foot 2x4; if you are working alone, use one long 2x4 cut at one end with a 45-degree angle to hold the first truss in place. These braces will hold the trusses up as you position them and check them for plumb.

To install the trusses, drive screws up into the bottom chord of each truss through the top plate, but you should also toenail the chords to the top plate. For extra-sturdy connections, use galvanized steel hurricane ties to attach the chords to the plates. Your local building department may actually require this. In any event, it provides a strong connection. Once the trusses are secured to the top plates and sheathed, you will have a good, sturdy roof that won't blow off in a high wind.

Building Trusses

1 With a truss laid out on the floor deck (obviously, before you have raised the walls), lay down a thick bead of construction adhesive and carefully lay the plywood gussets in place.

4 With the walls raised, position trusses so that they sit directly on top of the 2x4 studs. In this way, the load is carried cleanly from the roof to the foundation. Setting the first truss is the trickiest, but note that a long 2x4 cut with an angle at one end helps with the process.

2 With the gussets positioned so that the edges are flush with the edges of the 2x4 chords, nail them in place using roofing nails. You may want to trim the gussets to avoid sharp corners, but it's not necessary.

3 Each truss should have five gussets: one at both ends of the bottom chord; one at the peak of the truss; and one at each of the two junctures where the two roof pitches meet.

5 Each truss must be checked for plumb. As the truss is made plumb, it can be temporarily attached to the adjacent truss using 2x4 braces that will be removed later.

6 Screwing braces into place will hold the trusses until they are sheathed. The sheathing acts to stabilize the whole assembly. *(continued on page 82)*

(continued from page 81)

Building Trusses

7 For the end trusses, it is easiest to sheath them on the ground. Lay out two sheets of siding, and place the truss on top so that you can trace your cut lines.

8 After a truss has served as a guide for drawing cut lines, use a circular saw with the blade-depth set to exactly ½ in., and cut the T1-11 siding that will be attached to the end truss.

Prefabricated Trusses

Trusses can be ordered from your local lumberyard, but stick to standard dimensions: 8, 10, 12 feet, etc., increasing in increments of 2 feet each time. You can also specify the pitch. If the trusses that the lumberyard offers aren't to your liking, you can even have custom trusses made for you, though this will be far more costly than making them on-site by yourself using 2x4 lumber. Be sure to time truss delivery for when your walls are complete. Trusses are often delivered on a "scissor truck," which acts as an elevator. The truck can lift its bed up to your roofline and slide the finished trusses right off the truck and onto the top of your walls. This can save a lot of awkward and arduous lifting.

10 Mark the siding for placement of the louver vents (necessary for ventilating the shed), and then use a circular saw to create a rough opening in which to place the vents. There should be one vent on each end wall.

9 Screw the siding onto the 2x4 truss as you would attach any other sheathing, with screws every 6 in. around the perimeter chords.

11 To attach an end truss firmly to a wall, screw up through the wall top plate into the bottom of the truss's bottom chord. Use at least one screw per stud bay, or at least one screw every 16 in. in open areas.

12 For the rest of the trusses, screw down through the truss's bottom chord into the top plate at a diagonal. The random 2x4 braces that you see in place here will be removed once the roof is sheathed.

The Roofing

Most do-it-yourselfers can probably roof this shed in a matter of two or three hours, especially if you have a helper passing shingles up to you. Like any roof covered with asphalt shingles, this roof requires ½-inch CDX plywood sheathing and a minimum of #10 roofing felt. The 4-inch drip edge helps create a watertight seal at the edge of the plywood sheathing. (Note that in the photos shown here the 1x4 primed and painted trim was put in place along the soffit and rakes before the drip edge was installed.)

The roof on this gambrel shed has a hefty overhang all the way around the structure, keeping water away from the shed. Water is a real concern when you are using T1-11 siding; it must be kept as dry as possible. That's because T1-11 is made of plywood (or OSB), which can delaminate if it is exposed to a great deal of water. A good painted finish will also help protect the siding.

Applying Shingles. It is now widely recommended that roofers apply a course of shingles upside down all the way around the perimeter of the roof before applying the final shingles in the usual manner. This gives an extra seal where the top shingles come near the roof edge. Also note that where the pitch changes at midroof, a single course of shingles should overlap at midshingle, not at a break in courses. The shingle that spans this pitch transition will stick out for a while, and it may look rough at first, but as the sun heats the shingles, they will droop over and cover the pitch transition nicely.

Other Roofing Materials

Though asphalt shingles are inexpensive and easy to install, there are a number of other roofing products available. Let the type of roofing used on other buildings on your property and the shed's use guide your decision. The choices include cedar shakes; ag-panel, which is a ribbed metal material; and standing-seam metal roofs, which are highly durable and very attractive, but expensive. Metal roofs are usually installed by professionals.

Roofing the Shed

1 Like any roof, this gambrel roof can be sheathed with ½-in. CDX plywood. Nail the sheathing every 6 in. around its perimeter and every 8 in. along the truss chords in the interior of the panel.

3 Nail 4-in. drip edge in place using galvanized roofing nails. Drip edge can be cut easily using tin snips. It gives a good, clean, crisp look to the edge of the roof, while creating a seal between the roof and the soffit-and-rake trim.

2 The #10 roofing felt should be applied beneath the shingles before the drip edge is installed. Tack it in place using roofing nails or staples. Note that the 1x4 trim is already in place.

4 Install a course of shingles upside down—with the tabs facing in—to serve as an extra layer of protection beneath the shingles that break along the edge of the roof.

5 Three-tab shingles can be applied to any gambrel roof, just as they can be applied to a gable roof. Stagger the shingles so the seams of an upper course do not line up with the seams of the course beneath.

Front Wall and Door

The front of this gambrel shed is dominated by a large opening that will accommodate double shed doors. Although there is no need for a full-size header, such as that you would find over a door in your house, the door framing should consist of both king and jack studs that are nailed together firmly. Because the doors are rather heavy—they are nearly the size of a full 4x8 sheet of ½-inch plywood—they need the double-stud support. If the hinges were attached to just one stud and the door was pulled open, the stress could loosen the hinge screws or bow the framing.

And don't skimp on the cripple studs above the door opening. They maintain the 16-inch-on-center spacing that is required for proper attachment of the wall sheathing.

Build the Door. The door of the shed is made of a 2x4 frame sheathed with T1-11 siding. There is no need for diagonal bracing because once the T1-11 is attached to the frame using glue and screws, it is substantial enough to resist racking without additional support.

In our project, we applied the sheathing to the entire wall and then carefully cut out the opening. The section removed was used for the door. This method saves money but also requires some careful cutting.

To install the door hinges, lift the door in position and mark the locations for the hinges. With the surface hinges specified here, there is no need to cut a mortise for each hinge. With two people, one can hold the door in position while the other marks the hinge locations right on the door and the front wall of the shed. Attach the hinges to the door; double-check the hinge locations on the door frame; and attach the doors.

All the trim on this shed is 1x4 No. 2 pine. It is primed on both sides to seal it against moisture. Unfortunately, No. 2 pine contains a fair number of knots, so be sure to seal the knots with a good primer or sealer, otherwise the sap from the knots will quickly bleed through the finish paint. The paint job may look fine for a brief time, but in short order, you will begin to notice bleed through, especially if you use a latex paint.

Installing the Front Wall and Door

1 The rough opening for the shed doors has two studs on each side. This sturdy construction allows the shed to accommodate large swinging doors without worry that the weight of the doors will bow the framing.

4 Once the T1-11 has been cut away from the rough opening, glue and screw it to the 2x4 frame. The sheathing will prevent the frame from racking.

2 To create the doors, sheath right over the rough opening, as though it were a normal wall, and then—with the rough opening frame as your guide—carefully cut away the sheathing that will serve as the doors. Here, the shed has already been painted.

3 The door frame itself is made of 2x4 lumber. Because the T1-11 sheathing will be glued and screwed in place, the sheathing will provide substantial structural support for the door.

5 Once the sheathing has been attached to the 2x4 door frame, screw or nail in place 1x4 pine trim. Prime and paint the trim before attaching it to the door. It can be easily touched up once in place.

6 Install 1x4 trim to cover up any seams in the sheathing and on the corners. Trim out the shed's base and along the rake and soffits as well.

Final Touches

With the sheathing all properly nailed to prevent racking, it is time to apply the rest of the trim. Corner boards are an architectural element that bring a pleasing look to the shed. This shed has them on every corner, but not along the bottom of the long walls. By adding trim along the bottom of the sheathing, you box in the walls, creating the illusion that the shed is smaller than it really is, so avoid the bottom trim.

The luxury of T1-11 siding is that you do not have to apply another finish siding material, such as shingles or clapboard. Use a brush to paint the seams, which are really just the paths that an industrial router took to cut grooves in the siding, and then use a wide roller to apply paint to the rest of the paneling.

After the trim has been installed and the sheathing painted, it's time to build a platform, steps, or ramp up to the entry of the shed. Just as with the shed's foundation, 4-inch blocks can support a step or platform. With this finishing touch in place, the shed will have a nice finished look, with an entryway and double doors that swing wide to accommodate any activity or equipment that needs to be stored within.

Adding a Ramp

Though stairs or a platform are the most convenient and easy structural features to build in front of your shed, you may want to store a large piece of equipment such as a riding mower or rototiller. These items roll up ramps better than they climb stairs, so it's a good idea to have a ramp design in mind when building your shed, or at least be prepared to accommodate a removable ramp.

A temporary ramp can be made from something as simple as 2x6s laid in place when you need them. A more permanent ramp should be attached to the shed so that it does not move when in use. You may also need to build a more permanent foundation system that can take the constant movement on the ramp. The key is to be able to open the doors fully without having the swing of the doors blocked in any way. Make the ramp long enough to provide a gentle slope up to the shed.

Finishing

1 Using a brush, cut in the seams of the T1-11 so that the T1-11 sheathing can be easily painted using a thick roller. The raw wood is rather absorbent, so buy plenty of paint.

3 Dig pads for 4-in. solid cap blocks to serve as foundations for the steps or platform leading to the shed. The cap blocks must be level.

2 Even though you have plumbed walls and trusses along the way, it is still important to have a 4-ft. level handy to double-check plumb on the corner boards.

4 The platform will inevitably come in contact with the ground, so assemble it using pressure-treated wood. Here, 2x6s are used to create the platform on top of a 2x6 frame.

5 Once the 2x6 pressure-treated frame is assembled and set in place, check it for level. If it is not level, you can shim beneath the cap-block foundation using dirt or stone.

chapter 6

gable potting shed

Gable Potting Shed Diagram

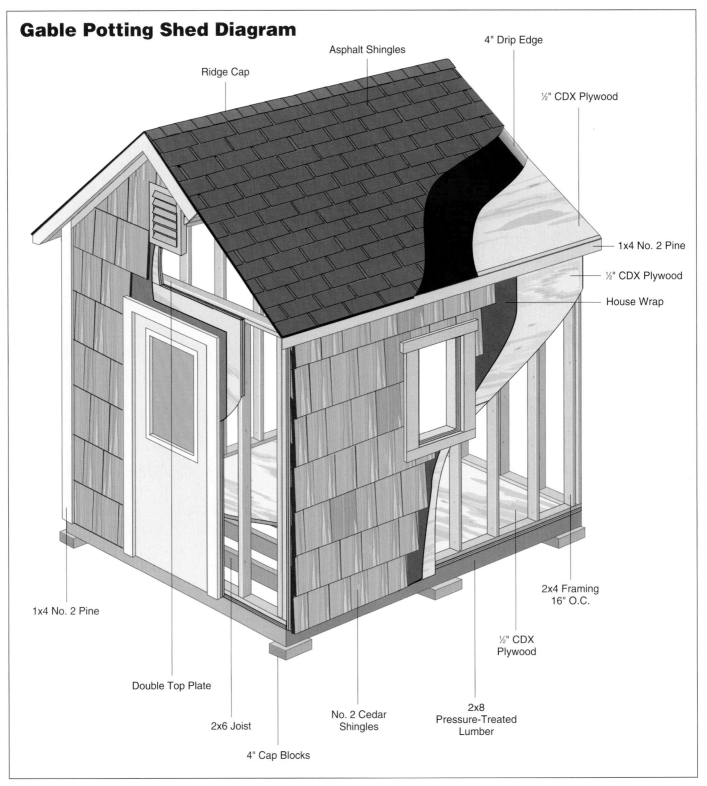

Ridge Cap

Asphalt Shingles

4" Drip Edge

½" CDX Plywood

1x4 No. 2 Pine

½" CDX Plywood

House Wrap

2x4 Framing 16" O.C.

½" CDX Plywood

1x4 No. 2 Pine

Double Top Plate

2x6 Joist

4" Cap Blocks

No. 2 Cedar Shingles

2x8 Pressure-Treated Lumber

Building the Gable Potting Shed

The 8 x 10-foot shed profiled in this chapter is an ideal multipurpose structure, and it can serve you over the course of a lifetime. Its gable roof—with a ridgeline that rises 14 feet above the ground—allows for a roomy loft for storage (or even sleeping if the shed serves as a club-house). The 80 square feet of space below leaves ample room for everything from a rider mower to a mini-workshop or potting and garden-tool area.

Framing Facts. Given the standard dimensions of this structure (8 feet wide, 8 feet tall, and 10 feet long), it is simple to build with very little cutting of standard dimension lumber. When ordering materials, specify 8- and 10-foot lengths, with one 12-foot 2x8 for the ridgeboard. Using standard dimension lumber will save you a great deal of cutting during the framing stages, and it cuts down on waste. Given that two sides of the shed are 8 feet long, framed with studs that are 16 inches on-center, you can use full sheets of plywood for sheathing. For the two 10-foot walls, 8-foot lengths of plywood will

cover all but 2 feet of the wall, but you can cut a single sheet of plywood to make up the difference.

The gable roof rises 4 feet above the wall's horizontal top plates, so a single sheet of plywood, notched for the exposed ridge beam, can cover each gable end.

The foundation of this shed is simple: solid block glued together in a

stack, sitting on top of gravel. In these photos, you'll see white gravel—actually marble chips. This is a purely aesthetic choice; standard ¾-inch gravel will do fine.

The 1x4 pine trim is nailed right to the underside of the soffit. With this design, you can extend the rafters beyond the walls and trim them plumb or leave them square.

Materials List

Foundation
3	50-lb bags of ¾" gravel
18	4" cap blocks
2 pcs.	2x8 10' pressure treated
4 pcs.	2x4 10' pressure treated
10 pcs.	2x6 8' pressure treated
12 tubes	construction adhesive

Framing and Sheathing
15 sheets	½" CDX plywood
42 pcs.	2x4 8' SPF
16 pcs.	2x6 8' SPF
1 pc.	2x8 12' SPF
2 louver vents	16" x 20"

1 roll	house wrap
10d common nails	
8d common nails	
2½" coated screws	

Roofing
8 pcs.	4" drip edge
1	100' roll #10 roofing felt
6 bundles	packs of 3-tab shingles
⅞" roofing nails	

Trim and Siding
17 pcs.	1x4 8' No. 2 pine
10 bundles	No. 2 cedar shingles

2½" galvanized finishing nails	
1 gal.	cedar sealer
1 gal.	primer for trim
1 gal.	paint for trim

Doors and Windows
1 prehung door	
2 windows	36" x 40"
1 pack cedar shims	

Stairs
6 pcs.	4" cap blocks
2 pcs.	2x6 10' pressure treated
10 pcs.	2x8 8' pressure treated

The Floor

Creating a straight footprint with square corners is essential. A ½-inch variation from corner to corner may not seem like much of a problem, but the discrepancy will express itself later as gaps in sheathing or a ridgeboard that isn't level.

Building on a Hilly Site

Though a good level site is desirable, it's rare to find a perfect grade for your shed. Luckily, the force exerted by the weight of a shed is a load that bears straight down, so stacked blocks can serve as a "foundation." There is no need to excavate for and pour concrete footings or walls.

When making a foundation for a hilly site, first excavate on the "high" side of the shed's footprint, and install a set of single blocks on ¾-inch gravel, dug to a depth that protects against frost heaving. (See "Block Foundations," page 26.) For the 10-foot run of this shed's rim joist (the joist that runs along the long wall), three sets of blocks will do— one at each end and one at the midpoint. For the 8-foot run, just two sets are required.

With the blocks on the high side set and level, place a 4-foot level on a straight 8-foot-long 2x4 board, and raise or lower the board until you find the approximate height of the blocks on the downhill side of your shed. Excavate pads for these downhill blocks, and fill the pads with gravel so that you achieve the desired elevation, always calculating in 4-inch, full-block increments.

Once the blocks are set and level, check the foundation for square. The corner-to-corner distance should match the corner-to-corner distance of the corresponding set of blocks.

Framing the Floor

1 With the 2x8 rim joist in place, a 2x4 ledger board provides a good bearing surface for the 2x6 joists. Using a tape measure, lay out the location for those joists so that they are 16 in. on center.

4 Glue decking to the joists using a good thick bead of standard construction adhesive. Although the floor sheathing will be screwed in place, the adhesive gives structural stability to the shed and keeps the floor from squeaking when you walk on it.

2 Set 2x6 pressure-treated joists in place, leaving the rim joist's end grain exposed. You may need to shim floor joists so that they are flush with the top of the rim joist.

3 Use a framing square to make sure that each 2x6 joist is perfectly square to the rim joints. Once the floor decking is installed, you will depend on this standard spacing to determine your nailing schedule.

5 Once sheathing is installed, square it up flush to the outside of the rim joists and snap chalk lines to establish guiding lines to help you locate where to screw the deck in place.

6 Using chalk lines as your guide, drive 2½-in. coated screws to attach the floor to the joists. Place screws every 6 in. around the perimeter and every 8 in. in the interior of the sheet.

The Walls

Wall framing is fun and remarkably easy to master for a simple structure like this 8 x 10-foot shed. The four walls of this shed can be easily framed, sheathed, and erected in one day. It's best to do this work with two people, because lifting a 10-foot wall that's been framed and sheathed will strain even a strong back. But it can be done solo. (If you're working alone, consider erecting the framed wall and sheathing it, one sheet at a time, after you have erected and plumbed the frame.)

Framing Options

Because this shed will never be insulated, the walls are framed with 2x4s, spaced 16 inches on center. To maintain the spacing, see "Laying Out the Walls," on page 39. If you intend to insulate your shed or want added structural stability (especially against high wind), use 2x6 studs framed 24 inches on center because the added depth will provide more room for insulation.

Sheathing. The sheathing is ½-inch CDX plywood, which is a low-grade and inexpensive plywood that is rough on both sides. It is not a suitable finish material. CDX affords more than enough structural stability against racking (wobbly side-to-side motion) of a building, but there is no need to glue the CDX sheathing to the wall studs as we did with the floor. Just nail it every 6 inches around the perimeter and every 8 inches along the studs in the interior of each sheet. There is no need to use screws, though they offer a better wood-to-wood connection.

Windows and Doors. Do not precut rough openings before nailing the sheathing to the stud walls, whether you install sheathing with the walls lying on the floor deck or erect. It is very easy to cut out the rough openings once the walls are erected and sheathed. To create indicator points, drill through from the inside of the shed at the corners of the rough opening. You can then run chalk lines from mark to mark to frame the openings. Then plunge-cut with a circular or reciprocating saw.

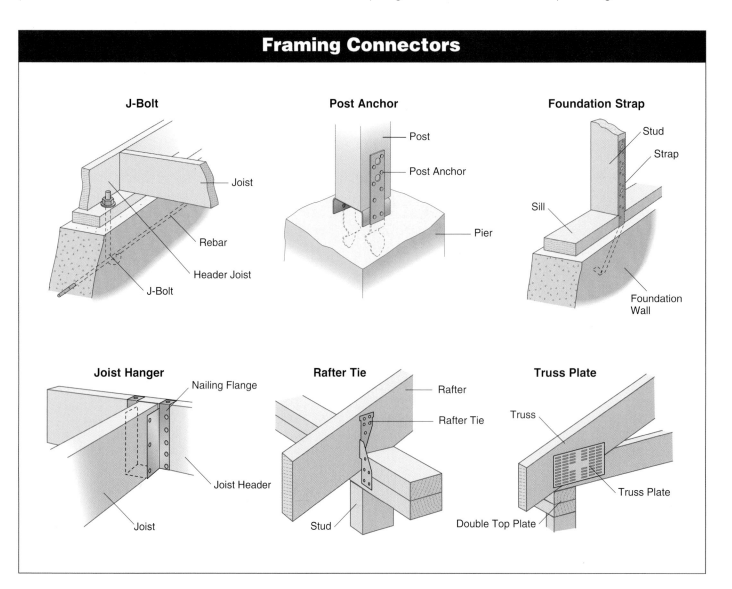

Framing Connectors

J-Bolt
- Joist
- Rebar
- Header Joist
- J-Bolt

Post Anchor
- Post
- Post Anchor
- Pier

Foundation Strap
- Stud
- Strap
- Sill
- Foundation Wall

Joist Hanger
- Nailing Flange
- Joist Header
- Joist

Rafter Tie
- Rafter
- Rafter Tie
- Stud

Truss Plate
- Truss
- Truss Plate
- Double Top Plate

Framing the Walls

1 With a 10-ft.-long 2x4 soleplate set in place near the edge of the floor, mark off 16-in. on-center lines to guide the placement of studs.

2 Drive home two nails per stud to connect studs to the top and bottom plates. End nailing ensures a good stud to plate connection.

3 Sheathe stud walls while they sit on the floor deck by spacing nails every 6 in. around the perimeter and every 8 in. in the interior.

4 Overlap the sheathing by 2 in. so that when the wall is erected, the overlap covers and protects the connection between the soleplate, the floor decking, and the rim joist. *(continued on page 96)*

(continued on page 96)

(continued from page 95)

Framing the Walls

5 With a brace in place, you can move the wall back and forth until you achieve plumb. When erecting first walls, have temporary 2x4 braces ready to support the wall once it is plumb.

6 When laying out a wall, a rough opening is defined by a king stud and a jack stud. The king stud extends from the soleplate to the top plate, but the jack stud supports a header at the top of the rough opening.

8 To determine the corners of an opening, use a 1-in. spade bit to drill through from the inside at the four corners of the rough opening. With a 1-in. hole at each corner, it's easy to "connect the dots" using a reciprocating or circular saw and remove the section.

9 The corners of a rough opening can be cleaned up using a power saber saw. A ratty corner that isn't square will block the smooth installation of a window.

7 Nail king and jack studs in place, just as you would any other stud. Note that the jack stud needs to bear against the horizontal header that defines the top of the rough opening. Otherwise it will be hard to nail firmly.

Ventilation

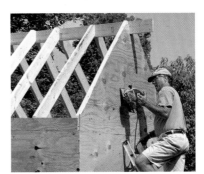

A gable vent will help keep the shed cool and expel stale air from inside the shed. To install the vent, mark and plunge-cut a rough opening at the center of the gable-end wall. There is no need to frame a rough opening. A vent is light enough to be glued and screwed directly to the sheathing.

10 After rough openings are cut out, the sheathing can be removed and saved for other parts of the project. A good, clean rough opening is essential for proper placement of windows and doors.

11 Nail or screw through the soleplate, but don't nail the soleplate where doorways occur as you will remove this section to install the door.
(continued on page 98)

(continued from page 97)

Framing the Walls

12 Position studs 16 in. apart, even when they do not run all the way to the top plate. As you sheathe the structure, this standard spacing of 16 in. on center will allow sheathing to break directly on studs.

13 Even though studs must occur at 16 in. on center along the wall, rough openings may call for studs to occur at nonstandard intervals.

16 Once a stud wall is in place, nail the end studs into the end studs of the adjacent walls, at least every 12 in. Use a 4-ft. level to check for plumb as you work.

17 With the stud wall plumbed and nailed into adjacent walls, nail through the soleplate into the rim joist for a good connection. Do not depend on nailing through the floor decking alone to establish a sound framing connection.

14 Nail a stop board on the outside of the stud walls you have lifted into place. When adjacent walls are erected, this stop will keep the new wall from toppling over.

15 Erect walls so that they are plumb and square. One person can easily lift an 8 x 10-ft. 2x4 wall without sheathing in place.

18 On unsheathed walls, attach ½-in. plywood sheathing. Drive nails every 6 in. on the perimeter of the sheet and every 8 in. in the interior.

19 Once the four walls are erected and sheathed, tie the walls together by installing a second top plate that overlaps adjacent walls at the corners. Drive two nails for each stud bay.

Roof Framing

The geometry and math of roof framing can boggle the minds of mere mortals. But for a simple gable roof like the one on this shed, you can avoid all the math by setting the ridgeboard, marking and cutting a "master rafter" by holding and marking a 2x6 in place, and then using the master to cut the remaining rafters. Note that in this shed design, the ridgeboard is 12 feet long and hangs beyond both end walls to create 1-foot gable overhangs. (See "Gable Framing," page 43.)

Getting Started. Though rafter framing is the most challenging aspect of this shed project, it can be managed by breaking down the steps. First, using a 2x4, place a brace board at each end of the shed. The braces run from the ground to a height 4 feet above the top plate. Position the poles so that the edge of each pole is ¾ inch to the right of the midpoint of the shed wall as you stand facing the wall. In other words, the two braces should be on opposite sides of the midpoint. (Compare photos 1 and 2.)

Attach the ridgeboard flush with the tops of the braces. Make sure the ridgeboard is set between the two poles. If the poles are plumb, the ridgeboard should be level and directly above the midpoint of the shed. Nonetheless, check the ridgeboard for level; a ridge with even a 1-inch slope across 10 feet will look out of whack to the naked eye. Mark the ridgeboard for 16-inch-on-center rafter locations.

Adding Rafters. Once the ridgeboard is set, hold the master rafter in place. You can make seat cuts in the rafters if you want to extend them beyond the shed wall to create an overhang, or you can cut the edge of the rafter at an angle so that it bears on the top plate as shown here.

With the master rafter as your template, gang-cut the other rafters. Then install two rafters at either end of the ridgeboard. The rafters should bear directly over the studs.

Apply roof sheathing by starting at the bottom of the roof and working toward the ridge, creating an 18-inch overhang at the eaves. Nail sheathing every 6 inches along panel ends and 12 inches in the interior of each panel.

Framing the Roof

1 With braces installed to hold the ridgeboard, temporarily nail the ridgeboard flush with the tops of the braces. Just one nail at each end is all that is required at this point.

4 Toenail the rafters to the top plate, nailing at least one nail in from each side. A band of wall sheathing will help to stabilize these rafters.

2 Check the ridgeboard for level. Because the ridge beam is attached to each brace by just one nail, you can make adjustments with ease. Also check to make sure the ridge rises 4 ft. above the top plate.

3 Before removing the braces, set the end rafters in place to stabilize the ridgeboard. The end rafters should be flush against the end of the top plates so that sheathing is flush to the stud walls and rafters.

5 Gable studs will fill in the triangle created by the gable-end rafters. These gable studs will provide a nailing surface 16 in. on center for the sheathing.

6 Check gable studs for plumb, but note that the gable-end studs are not truly a structural component of the wall; these studs serve as a nailing surface for gable sheathing.

Doors and Windows

Wrapping your shed in a semipermeable house wrap is a good construction practice. House wrap isn't that expensive and is easy to install, and it provides a wind shield while allowing moisture that accumulates inside the shed to migrate to the outside. House wrap is especially good at sealing up rough openings because it is applied before windows and doors are inserted. For best results, wrap the material around all rough openings.

Installing windows and doors in the shed provides temporary protection against the weather. But note that plywood, even with house wrap covering it, is not designed for sustained contact with the elements. So even after installing house wrap and inserting windows and doors, move directly to the installation of permanent siding and roofing to fully weatherproof the new building.

Doors. For a project like this, use prehung doors. In fact, it may be a good idea to find a door you like and use its measurements to create the rough opening size.

It takes advanced carpentry skills to build a doorjamb from stock lumber. Prehung doors are affordable, but more important, they have factory edges and quality connections. You won't regret installing a prehung door, but you may well curse the day you decided to build a doorjamb from scratch to save $100.

Windows. Though many windows come with brick molding and factory-made jambs, you do not need that style of finished window for a shed. You can save money by buying a window unit without exterior trim. Slide the window unit into the rough opening; make sure it is plumb and level, using shims if necessary; and use screws to attach it directly to the studs that form the rough opening. To finish, frame the face of the window, inside and out, with 1x4 No. 2 pine stock. The trim looks good and helps to trap the window in place.

After applying trim to the windows, it is a good idea to nail up the 1x4 trim on the gable and the eaves.

Installing Doors and Windows

1 Roll out house wrap so it is taut, and staple it in place every 12 in. or so. Overlap courses by 6 in. Once you start a course, run it as long as possible, wrapping it all the way around the shed.

4 With the rough opening crisply defined by taut house wrap stapled inside and out, install the prehung door and shim it behind each hinge. Nail through the brick molding, and nail directly through the shims to connect the doorjamb with the framing.

2 For rough openings, use a razor knife to cut an "X" pattern in the house wrap. Don't overcut the wrap at the corners because that defeats the sealing effect of the wrap after the window is inserted.

3 Once the house wrap has been cut in an "X" pattern, fold or roll it back neatly, and staple it to the side of the studs that define the rough opening.

5 Once a window is inserted in a rough opening, shim it using cedar shingles until it is plumb and level. Drill through the shims to create a solid connection between the window, the shims, and the framing.

6 Later, you will trim windows with 1x4 No. 2 pine. Using galvanized finishing nails, fasten the trim to the shed by nailing through the sheathing into the framing.

Siding and Trim

When it is time to trim and side your shed, you can really start to envision the finished project. Trim out the shed before you add siding because the siding will abut the trim, creating nice clean lines.

For trimming corners, around windows, and the rakes and eaves, use 1x4 No. 2 pine. Though this grade has some knots, the knots can be sealed using a sealer, and you will save the substantial cost of using clear (knot-free) pine. For a really smooth finish, sand the boards using 100-grit sandpaper before sealing the knots, and then apply two coats of exterior semi-gloss latex paint. (For a really smooth finish, sand between coats of paint.) It is highly advisable to paint the trim boards before you install them, even if you have to go back to touch up scuffs and hammer marks. Painting trim boards in place is time-consuming, especially around cedar siding, where you have to cut in along the edge of the shingles.

Attach the rake and eave trim by screwing down through the roof sheathing. For the eave trim, rip a 45-degree miter along the edge of the board so that it fits neatly under the roof sheathing. Be sure to level and plumb trim boards, because even a small variation from level or plumb can be picked up by the naked eye.

There is no need to glue corner-board trim, because you would be gluing the boards just to the house wrap—not the sheathing.

1 The rake board is the trim piece that is attached to the underside of the gable overhang. Use construction adhesive to glue the trim into place, and attach it by screwing down through the roof sheathing.

3 Exterior trim made of 1x4 No. 2 pine is ideal for most sheds. The corner boards can be mitered at the top so that they fit snugly. A little exterior-grade caulk to seal up this joint may be required.

4 Attach corner boards by using the corner of the shed as your guide. If the walls are plumb and the foundation level, the trim boards will be plumb as well. But it's always good to double-check using a 4-ft. level.

2 Prepaint all wall trim boards; you can touch up scuffs later. First, sand the boards, and then seal the knots. Set up trim boards on sawhorses, with 2x4 outriggers, so you can use a roller to paint lots of boards at once.

5 Attach trim to the shed wall under the overhang, using galvanized finishing nails. You can install soffit trim or leave the soffits open.

The Roof

Roofing is tricky when you have to contend with valleys and odd angles where roof planes meet. But with a gable roof, like the one on this shed, installing three-tab asphalt shingles is a cinch, even for beginners. First, install #10 roofing felt (very lightweight tar paper) to cover all the roof sheathing. If you are going to install shingles right away, this roofing felt can be held in place using staples or roofing nails. But if you are not installing shingles immediately, attach the roofing felt using circular nail-in-place fasteners designed just for this task (available where you buy shingles). This gives the felt more holding power in strong winds, but it is best to apply roofing as soon as possible.

As you install roofing felt, you may want to nail in place temporary cleats as a safety measure when shingling. These can be removed as you work on the roof.

Once the roof felt is in place, install 4-inch drip edge. Drip edge really tidies up the roof edge, hiding the ratty edge where the roofing felt laps the end of the roof sheathing. Trim the drip edge to length using snips, and nail it using galvanized roofing nails. The rake and soffit trim should be in place before the drip edge.

With the drip edge in place, install a course of shingles, "upside down," with the three tabs on the uphill side of the roof. The upside-down starter course protects the underside of the first true course of shingles, where the gaps occur between tabs. It used to be recommended that this upside-down shingle course be installed just across the bottom edge of the roof, but it is a better practice to run this upside-down course all the way around the perimeter of your roof.

6 Gable Potting Shed

To apply finished shingles, start in a corner, and nail a course of shingles all the way across the full length of the roof. Once that is in place, install the second course, but start the first shingle with a "half-lap" so the gaps between the tabs don't line up with the course below. This practice will require that you run the shingles temporarily "wild" at the end of the roof. Trim shingles with a sharp razor knife by cutting the underside, using the edge of the roof sheathing as your guide.

Ridge caps are made from shingles. Simply cut a 3-tab asphalt shingle into three separate tabs. Each tab is a ridge cap. Install ridge caps by leaving exposed just the granular aspect of the shingle. For the final ridge cap, cut it in half widthwise so that you are nailing in place just the granular half of the shingle. Dab roofing adhesive on the nailheads left exposed on this last "half-tab" ridge cap. To get a good finish on ridge caps and avoid bulging, trim the part of the shingle that will be covered (the nongranular half of the tab) so that it forms an "A" shape. The A-shape allows the next shingle to fold over it without creating a bulge.

Roofing the Shed

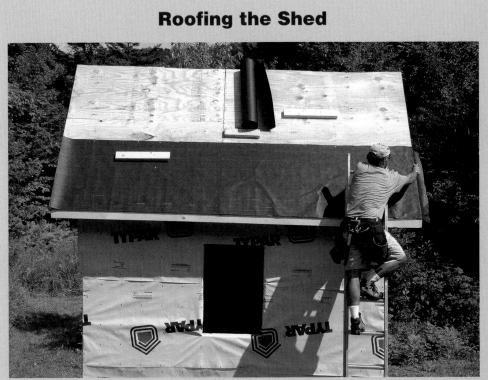

1 Apply roofing felt across the entire roof before shingling. Overlap any seams by 6 in., and trim the edges using a sharp razor knife. Stapling will hold the roofing felt in place if you are installing shingles right away.

4 Before installing finished shingles, install an upside-down "under course" of shingles—with the tabs facing in—all the way around the perimeter of the roof. This protects the gap beneath the tabs of the first course.

5 As you work up from the bottom of the roof, each successive course of shingles must have the tabs staggered by half a tab. This ensures that the gaps between tabs in the shingles do not line up with the gaps of the shingles below.

2 Along the gable end and along the soffit, a 4-in. drip edge really adds a nice neat look to the edge of the roof. Note that the rake and soffit trim boards must be in place for the drip edge to be installed properly.

3 Trim drip edge using sharp snips. There is no need to miter the ends of the drip edge. The drip-edge pieces simply overlap one another. Nail them in place using standard galvanized roofing nails.

6 Allow shingles to hang temporarily "wild" over the edge of the roof, and then trim them by cutting with a sharp razor knife across the underside of the shingle. Do not cut the shingles from the top, granular side. It will dull the razor very quickly.

7 Ridge caps are made by cutting up the 3-tab shingles into three individual tabs. Overlap ridge caps so that just the granular half of the tab is exposed. Dab nailheads with roofing cement.

Building Steps

The shed's entryway can be as elaborate as a stairway with handrails or as simple as a platform made of pressure-treated wood. In all cases, level the rim joists, just as you did with the rim joists for the shed's foundation. Build a box to size; then attach 2x6 pressure-treated planks to the joists.

When positioning 2x6 pressure-treated decking planks, leave enough room between them—about ½ in.—to allow standing water to drain.

Finishing the Shed

1 Siding with cedar shingles is fun, though time-consuming, because as each course ends, you may have to custom-cut shingles using a razor knife to bring the course flush up against the corner boards.

4 Some shingle courses may have shingles that are just 4 in. tall. These must be nailed in place using galvanized finishing nails because there will be no course laid on top to cover the exposed nailheads.

2 Getting the first course level is crucial. After the first course is in place, measure up to the bottom of the next course, and this course-to-course distance must be maintained for the entire structure.

3 Shingling under windows may require that you cut off the tops of some shingles to make them fit. Trim as needed to maintain the exposure established below.

5 Seal knots on all pine trim because the sap from knots will invariably bleed through most finish paints, leaving unsightly brown circles. You will have to discard the brush you use for sealant, so pick an old one you don't mind throwing away.

glossary

Backfill Soil or gravel used to fill in between a foundation or retaining wall and the ground excavated around it.

Barge rafters The last outside rafters of a structure. They are usually nailed to outriggers and form the gable-end overhangs.

Battens Narrow wood strips that cover vertical joints between siding boards.

Bird's mouth The notch made of a level and plumb cut near the tail end of a rafter where the rafter edge rests on a top plate or horizontal framing member.

Blocking Lumber added between studs, joists, rafters, or other framing members to provide a nailing surface, additional strength, spacing between boards, or firestopping.

Chord The wood members of a truss that form the two sides of the roof and the base, or ceiling joist.

Cleat A small board fastened to a surface to provide support for another board, or any board nailed onto another board to strengthen or support it.

Collar tie A horizontal board installed rafter-to-rafter for extra support.

Corner boards Boards nailed vertically to the corners of a building that serve as a stopping point for siding and as an architectural feature.

Cripple studs Short studs that stand vertically between a header and top plate or between a bottom plate and the underside of a rough sill.

Dead load The weight of a building's components, including lumber, roofing, and permanent fixtures.

Easement The legal right for one person to cross or use another's land. The most common easements are narrow tracts for utility lines.

Eaves The lower part of a roof that projects beyond the supporting walls to create an overhang.

Face-nailing Nailing perpendicularly through the surface of lumber.

Fascia One-by or two-by trim pieces nailed onto the end grain or tail end of a rafter to form part of a cornice or overhang.

Flashing Thin sheets of aluminum, copper, rubber asphalt, or other material used to bridge or cover a joint between materials that is exposed to the weather.

Floor joists The long wooden beams generally set horizontally 16 inches on center between foundation walls or girders.

Footing The part of a foundation that transmits loads to the soil.

Frost line The maximum depth to which soil freezes in winter.

Full stud Vertical two-by lumber that extends from the bottom plate to the top plate of a wall.

Gable end The triangular wall section under each end of a gable roof.

Gambrel roof A roof design that combines two gable roofs of differing slopes.

Grade The identification class of lumber quality. Also shorthand for ground level—the finished level of the ground on a building site.

Gusset plates Metal or plywood plates used to hold together the chords and webs of a truss.

Header The thick horizontal member that runs above rough openings, such as doors and windows, in a building's frame.

Header joist A horizontal board, installed on edge, that is secured to the ends of the floor joists.

Jack stud A stud that runs from the bottom plate to the underside of a header. Also called a trimmer.

Joist Horizontal framing lumber placed on edge to support subfloors or hold up ceilings.

Joist hanger Bracket used to strengthen the connection between a joist and a piece of lumber into which it butts.

Kerf The narrow slot a saw blade cuts in a piece of lumber, usually about ⅛ inch thick.

Live load All loads in and on a building that are not a permanent part of the structure—such as furniture, people, and wind.

Miter A joint in which two boards are joined at angles (usually 45 degrees) to form a corner.

Nailing flange An extension attached to a building component, usually predrilled for nails or screws.

Nominal dimensions In lumber, the premilling measurement for which a piece of lumber is named (i.e., 2x4); in masonry, the measured dimensions of a masonry unit plus one mortar joint.

O.C. An abbreviation for on center, typically referring to layout measurements taken from the center of one stud to the center of the next stud.

Oriented-strand board (OSB) Panel material made of wood strands purposely aligned for strength and bonded together with adhesive.

Outrigger A projecting framing member run out from a main structure to provide additional stability or nailing for another framing component.

Pilot hole A hole drilled before a screw is inserted to defeat splitting.

Pitch Loosely, the slope or angle of a roof.

Platform framing The framing method in which walls are built one story at a time on top of decked platforms over the story below.

Plumb Vertically straight. A line 90 degrees to a level line.

Prehung door A door that's already set in a jamb, with hinges (and sometimes a lockset) pre-assembled, ready to be installed in a rough opening.

Rake trim Trim boards applied to the fascia along the gable ends of a roof projection.

Ridgeboard The horizontal board that defines the roof frame's highest point, or ridge.

Ridge cut The cut at the uphill end of a rafter, along the ridge plumb line, that allows the rafter's end grain to sit flush against the ridgeboard.

Rim joists Joists that define the outside edges of a platform.

Scarf joint Where the end grain of two pieces of lumber meet in the same plane at a 45-degree angle, or in a jagged, overlapped cut, typically backed up by another board or hardware to secure the joint.

Setback A local building code that requires structures to be built a certain distance from the street, sidewalk, or property line.

Sheathing Panel material, typically plywood, applied to the outside of a structure. Siding is installed over it.

Shed roof A roof that slopes in one direction.

Sill The horizontal two-by lumber attached directly to the masonry foundation. It supports the building's walls.

Soffit The boards or plywood panels that run the length of a wall on the underside of the rafters, covering the space between the wall and the fascia.

Soleplate The horizontal two-by lumber that forms the base of framed walls, also called a shoe.

Toenailing Driving a nail at an angle into the face of a board so that it penetrates another board beneath or above it.

Top plate The horizontal two-by board nailed to the top of wall studs, almost always consisting of two boards that overlap at the corners.

Truss A rigid assembly of timbers relying on tri-angulation to span distances impractical for a single member.

Valley flashing Material used to prevent leaks at the intersection of two pitched roofs that form an internal angle.

Web The inner members of a truss that carry loads from the chords, or perimeter members.

Z-brace door Door construction typically consisting of boards joined together and strengthened by a series of braces screwed to the backs of the boards in a Z-shaped pattern.

index

index

photo credits